SHELLI JONES BAKER

McDougal Publishing is a ministry of The McDougal Foundation, Inc., a Maryland nonprofit corporation dedicated to spreading the Gospel of the Lord Jesus Christ to as many people as possible in the shortest time possible.

Published by:

McDougal Publishing
P.O. Box 3595
Hagerstown, MD 21742-3595
www.mcdougalpublishing.com

ISBN 1-58158-016-9

Printed in the United States of America
For Worldwide Distribution

DEDICATION

I dedicate this book to my
faithful husband,
REV. RONNIE LEE BAKER

   With unwavering patience and ability to forbear my many hours spent on the road and in the studio, Ronnie has been a "Rock of Gibraltar" for me. His strength in prayer and encouragement are the backbone of this ministry.

Pastors Ronnie and Shelli Baker

ACKNOWLEDGMENTS

I would like to thank Jim and Judy Baker for their gift of hospitality as this manuscript was being prepared; Ashley, my young friend, your typing skills were a treasure; White Horse Christian Center, gratitude beyond words flows from my heart toward Pastor Jeff Johns and his staff of intercessors. This would not have been possible without all of you.

May God bless those torch carriers who have urged us on: Bob Shattles, Ruth Heflin, Gwen Shaw, Mama Mary Jenkins, Billye Brim, Flo Ellers and Carol Granderson. We are grateful to Jim and Kathy Kaseman, Steve and Muriel Johnson, Donna Nelson, Bill and Connie Wilson, Lee and Jan Morgans, Tredwell and Carole Lewis, Bertie McCoy, Sandy Robbins, Brad and Susie Stein, Tom and Sharon Arnold, the National Day of Prayer Committee in Philadelphia, TBN-TV 14 in Oklahoma City, my parents, Kathy and David Jones, and the staff of McDougal Publishing.

God bless all of our friends and supporters, especially Dottie, Debra, Bob, Angie and the "pray-ers" in Oklahoma City and Tulsa, for their many hours of planning behind the scenes for our revivals. Thanks for the mail runs, Kitty.

I want to thank Ronnie and our new church in Mansfield, Missouri (Harvest Projects International Revival Center), for excusing me to preach in other churches so often.

I must also thank Ruby Caudill, Sue Cox, Carolyn Metcalf and Lee Sharp, for keeping open a lifeline with the throne room.

Thanks to Pastors Nicholas and Qui Lin Wu of Christian Life Center, for their help in promoting the book in Malaysia.

CONTENTS

FOREWORDS

I have known Shelli Baker for several years now, but I would say that within the past six months God has put within her an ability to see performed in her ministry the miracles she has always longed for, but known only in measure. She recently came and spent a day with me, and she told me of miracle after miracle that God was doing in her meetings, and all were unusual creative miracles. Fourteen people, for instance, had received new knee joints. This is surely the time for the *Oceans of Glory* of which she writes so eloquently.

Shelli Baker sees the coming *Oceans of Glory*, not only as a potential for herself and her own ministry, but she sees them as a potential for *your* life and *your* ministry as well. As you read this book, your faith level will rise, and you will find yourself walking in greater expectation of what God is doing in this hour in the glory.

Ruth Ward Heflin
Ashland, Virginia
June 2000

Oceans of Glory speaks of Shelli's experience, vision and passion. There is a day coming when God will unleash the greatest move ever and Shelli is preparing the Church to move into that. I believe that this book will cause the reader to have a better understanding of God's great move in the last days.

Nicholas Wu
Christian Life Center
Malaysia
September 2000

INTRODUCTION

In October of 1998, the Lord told me to study everything I could about oceans. He told me to begin to proclaim that although the river movement was experiencing an ebbing tide, *Oceans of Glory* would now sweep in upon us and carry us to new depths, from which we could never return. Since that time, I have been challenging musicians to fast and pray to receive ocean songs from the Lord, to be able to hear a unique sound from Heaven for the revival in their own localities.

In February of 1999, at White Horse Christian Center in West Lafayette, Indiana, the Holy Spirit told me to fully release this message that had been building in my spirit since 1998. A "gusher" of glory was released in that place, as Pastor Jeff Johns gave me full liberty to proclaim this message, and Jayna Mullins, the worship leader in the church, picked up the theme and received a new song from the Lord — "Tsunami!" Assistant Pastor Johnny Beard led us all in a fiery dance of the Spirit until tsunami-sized waves of glory flooded over us, and absolutely everyone left in the place was slain in the Spirit and lay upon the floor for the next six hours.

Now, for the first time, this message is released in book form, and I trust that the same power of God that is being experienced in many places throughout the earth will flood the souls of all those who read these pages. May God's *Oceans of Glory* sweep over YOU today.

Shelli Jones Baker
Branson, Missouri

Afterward he brought me again unto the door of the house; and, behold, waters issued out from under the threshold of the house eastward: for the forefront of the house stood toward the EAST, and the waters came down from under from the right side of the house, at the SOUTH side of the altar.

Then brought he me out of the way of the gate northward, and led me about the way without unto the utter gate by the way that looketh eastward; and, behold, there ran out waters on the right side. And when the man that had the line in his hand went forth eastward, he measured a thousand cubits, and he brought me through the waters;

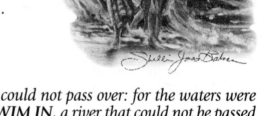

The waters were
TO THE ANKLES. ...
The waters were
TO THE KNEES. ...
The waters were
TO THE LOINS. ...

*It was a river that I could not pass over: for the waters were risen, **WATERS TO SWIM IN**, a river that could not be passed over.*   Ezekiel 47:1-5

For the earth shall be filled with the knowledge of the glory of the LORD, as the waters cover the sea.   Habakkuk 2:14

PROLOGUE

In 1987, the presence of God rushed in upon my hands and mind as I was working on my painting *The Travail of the Flag*. I had been at work on the twelve-foot mural for three months already, and although the spirit was willing to continue to pull the prophetic vision to earth through the point of the brush, my flesh had become weary. Colors on the pallet began to run together like mud at night, as I jabbed the brush at the canvas for the millionth time.

"Which color now, Lord?" I mused, "They're all starting to look the same. I need Your grace to finish this in time for the unveiling."

Turning to the work one more time, I seemed to fall into a refreshing trance. I worked on, not noticing either sunset or sunrise. I was laboring in the spirit of prayer and communion with the Master, and He created on the canvas an ocean of scenery.

The Travail of the Flag

Then, suddenly, as the brush reached the shoreline of the United States (as it was featured in the painting), I realized what had happened. Dropping the brush in awe, I began to worship the Lord. The entire ocean scene was complete, and it was beautiful. In it there were highlights of the blood of Jesus, of His glory and of the fire of the Spirit. And it all flowed from His side.

The Lord was poised over the far shore of Israel (on the other side of the mural), some five feet away from the spot where my brush had ended the task.

I was stunned. Who could ever paint the oceans of revival glory? Only under the guidance and inspiration of the Master Artist Himself could even the smallest glimpse of such a revelation be attempted.

9

How had I done it? Had angels helped? I wasn't sure. What I did know was that three days had passed from the moment of my cry, "Lord, give me grace to finish," and now the work was complete.

The painting of that ocean was a prophetic action, signaling things to come in the great revival of the twenty-first century, the great coming *Oceans of Glory.*

TSUNAMI! TIDAL WAVE!

Jesus answered, Verily, verily, I say unto thee, Except a man be born of water and of the Spirit, he cannot enter into the kingdom of God. That which is born of the flesh is flesh; and that which is born of the Spirit is spirit. Marvel not that I said unto thee, Ye must be born again. The wind bloweth where it listeth, and thou hearest the sound thereof, but canst not tell whence it cometh, and whither it goeth: so is every one that is born of the Spirit.
John 3:5-8

I hear a certain sound in the realm of the Spirit ... Be still ... Listen. What is it? ... A holy hush before the storm ...

Lapping waters, the whisper of a receding tide ... The river of God changes course, carrying us out to a greater depth, as the wind is pierced with prophetic warnings.

A voice cries, "Stay alert! Be watchful and prayerful in channels of deep waters! We're heading out to sea."

Another urges, "Beware of slow currents near the riverbank, ending in tidal pools, polluted already with new traditions!"

The calm is welcomed by some, but not by all.

Loss of momentum is a dangerous state to be in when one is in deep water. I hear a tremble in the distance ... What is it? ... Roaring ocean waves! A tsunami! A tidal wave of glory! The fountains of the deep are bursting on the horizon of a new millennium. We praised God for "the river," but what shall we do with the ocean?

The revival wave that is traveling toward us right now is like a tsunami at breakneck speed. It will come suddenly. It will flood an unsuspecting world, visiting all of its religious and nonreligious leaders alike. They may either panic or rejoice, but the spiritual wave is coming like the natural wave of Noah's day — whether we are ready for it or not. Tsunami! A sovereign move of God is upon us!

When this wave hits, everything in its path will be uprooted and changed. This great wave will come like a flash flood gushing down upon a dry river bed. Every pebble, now set in its place, will be moved and carried far downstream. People of stony hearts (set in their ways and attending to "business as usual") will instantly find their sedentary positions changed when this next visitation of God turns life topsy-turvy, upside down. The rocks of the flooded creek bed will be disturbed by boiling, churning waters of fire and glory rushing through.

Some are too busy to be revived. They would have to put God on their schedules first, but the revival waters of Heaven above will pour over their bounds like Niagara Falls — whether we have planned it or not. They will be caught by surprise.

This rush of glory will be white water from the top, and the height of its spray, rebounding from the force of its impact upon the sea of people below, will surpass the boundaries of its spilling. Rainbows of every biblical covenant promise of all the ages will dazzle and astound us as they are reflected in the mist of the glory cloud that moves across this planet:

> For the earth will be filled with the knowledge of the glory of the LORD, as the waters cover the sea. Habakkuk 2:14, NIV

 Waters to swim in! Waters to love God and man in! Birth waters of the womb of the Spirit, bringing new life!

> He that believeth on me, as the scripture hath said, out of his belly shall flow rivers of living water. John 7:38

Floods of possibility will soon flow to the heart of every dreamer ... *"exceedingly abundantly above all [he] can ask or think"*! No one can hold back an ocean, and all attempts to dam one up, as we do rivers, would be futile. This move of God will sweep the whole earth. As in the days of the great Welsh Revival, everyone, even the bartenders, will be busy with revival day and night. [1]

Whole towns are about to be flooded with *Oceans of Glory*! If it has happened before, it will happen again! You can count on it.

Just like surfers on the Pacific Ocean who, with that same assurance, calculate the approach of those coveted "monster" waves, we can get ready for this next one. This wave of revival glory will be "the motherlode"!

The tide of this ocean-sized revival has been here once before. It came two thousand years ago. Heralded by the sound of a *"rushing mighty wind,"* and with a "whoosh" of fiery power, a tsunami-sized wave of glory burst through the heavenlies suddenly, without warning (as tsunamis do)!

It first crashed into the lives of one hundred and twenty empty, praying vessels, who had been obeying Jesus' command to *"tarry"* in the Upper Room until the *"power"* should fall from on high. Instantly, this rush of power disoriented them, disrupted the natural order of their lives and rolled them like drunken men in the backwash of its outpouring. It carried them into the streets of Jerusalem to testify of God's overwhelming goodness.

As those fasting, praying vessels began to bubble with waters of the Holy Spirit, they poured forth in the language of the glory and gave drink to a thirsty humanity with words of jubilation and admonition for repentance. Mankind had not experienced this much glory since the day Adam had lost it in Eden — more than four thousand years before.

Power and immortality fled from man's soul and flesh when the glory departed, and its voice, which had whispered to every fiber of his being since the day he was created, "live and be blessed," was gone (see Hebrews 12:24-29). In the quake of the departure of the glory, Heaven shook, and earth groaned for the absence of the goodness that it once spoke.

Without the language of that glory in man's blood, the DNA of every cell was abandoned to reproduce without the full secret codes of life. Man's mind became void of critical wisdom needed to survive. But, Hallelujah! When God's glory reentered the earth at Pentecost, it was manifested once again through humans with power and purpose. The baptismal fires of glory brought anointings to proclaim God's goodness and to heal all manner of sickness and even to raise the dead. It was the first New Testament revival:

> Then Peter stood up with the Eleven, raised his voice and addressed the crowd: "Fellow Jews and all of you who live in Jerusalem, let me explain this to you; listen carefully to what I say. These men are not drunk, as you suppose. It's only nine in the morning! No, this is what was spoken by the prophet Joel:
>
> " 'In the last days, God says, I will pour out my Spirit on all people. Your sons and daughters will prophesy, your young men will see visions, your old men will dream dreams. Even on my servants, both men and women, I will pour out my Spirit in those days, and they will prophesy.
>
> "I will show wonders in the heaven above and signs on the earth below, blood and fire and billows of smoke. The sun will be turned to darkness and the moon to blood before the coming of the great and glorious day of the Lord. And everyone who calls on the name of the Lord will be saved.' "
>
> Acts 2:14-21, NIV

What an awesome gift! Who could contain the joy of it?

At Pentecost, the envelope of Heaven poured down love like liquid glory, and the roaring of its reentrance into the human race sounded like a *"rushing mighty wind"* to listening ears in Jerusalem. Where floodwaters of destruction had once ripped Heaven wide open in Noah's day, the glory tore it open again and out rushed oceans of blessing to a people trapped in the laws of judgment. Until then, they had only known God's Law, not His love.

The disciples were overwhelmed with feelings of shock and gratitude. The joy of it made them "drunk," and, with or without consent from others, they automatically became witnesses for God. When we know that what we have is real, nothing can hinder us from being bold and confident to demonstrate it and declare it to others. Soul-winning becomes as easy as a fresh sea breeze!

Can you imagine how Adam would have reacted had he been there that day? Oh, to experience a taste of the glory realm and fellowship with God, after having lost it!

 Soul-winning becomes as easy as a fresh sea breeze!

So many Christians have struggled throughout history with the guilt of being told to disciple all nations, while at the same time, having no power to win souls. Jesus did not plan for His followers to win souls apart from His glory. He prayed that God would glorify us — as He had *Him*. Jesus wanted us to have a flood of glory in our lives that would find its way into every nook and cranny of stone-cold hearts, in the same manner as floodwaters fill the crevices of a submerged city. No resistance or sandbag can keep out an ocean tidal wave.

God's *Oceans of Glory* sovereignly flooded Jerusalem on the Day of Pentecost. It was not just a trickle or a shallow stream. A tidal wave, a wall of God's presence, covered an entire city in a few moments' time, so that no one in Jerusalem was ignorant of the day's events by the time the sun had gone down.

As it was in Jerusalem, so shall it be in our cities; for that wave has moved throughout the earth, revisiting each ensuing generation on a cycle nearly as predictable as the passing of the comets. As the waves of the sea lap against the shore, bringing in the new and reclaiming what was before, tides of revival are rising once more.

As the waves of the sea lap against the shore, bringing in the new and reclaiming what was before, tides of revival are rising once more.

Patterns of Revival

It is exciting to see some recent cycles of revival waves retracing the same patterns, always hitting in the first year of the new century, such as those recorded in 1601, 1701, 1801 and 1901. The cycles flow like this: approximately five years before each revival, a period of unrest comes to religious and political circles, creating upheavals in the traditional systems, followed by a movement of repentance, followed by the outbreak of revival, miracles and change.

This pattern of revival was first brought to my attention by Rev. Paul Jehle, a historian and the pastor of the New Testament Church in Plymouth, Massachusetts, the site of our New England revival in 1999. [2] Seeing this obvious pattern encourages our expectation of revival with certainty. It will come. Understanding the pattern clarifies the focus of our prayers.

- 1500s: The Age of Discovery dawned, disturbing religious and political traditions. Martin Luther revived faith, rescuing God's written Word from its captivity in the Dark Ages.

- 1601: Government laws dictated the most minute details of how a person could pray — publicly and privately, from a common book of prayer. Spies betrayed violators. Separatists, however, defied the restrictions by praying out of their own hearts. This led to a wave of glorious awakening, followed by storms of bloody persecution. They exited that wave on a ship called the *Mayflower*. America was founded upon their zeal for prayer and their love for the Word of God. But the century ended with a backslidden third generation, engulfed in the hysteria of experience and superstition, superseding a firm foundation in the Word. The infamous result was the Salem witch trials. [3]

- 1701: Repentance began for the Salem witch trials, including fasting and prayer. This resulted in the First Great Awakening in 1734, which focused upon God's Word, with signs following, preparing the colonists for the Revolutionary War. The far-reaching influence of the revival even birthed a new and unique constitution for the United States of America.

- 1801: Presbyterians at Cane Ridge, Kentucky, brought multitudes back to Christ in waves of glory that mirrored those of the First Great Awakening before it, and of the recent River Movement at the close of the twentieth century. Crowds of twenty-five thousand (exceeding the entire population of the town) attended six days of revival that affected an entire century. Sounds of revival reminded one reporter from Niagara Falls of a mighty river. Fireballs of glory, like the head of a comet, made war on the sin of their carnal flesh. As they were slain in the Spirit for days under *Oceans of Glory*, God pressed them to purity of heart. And its heavenly force slayed five hundred upon the ground for three days. [4] More, Lord! Again!

Cane Ridge was followed by the Wesleyan Methodist Revival of Martha's Vineyard island in Massachusetts, which entertained hungry crowds of twenty thousand in annual summer campmeetings for half a century, also gloriously involving the native Indian population as well.

- 1901: The first day of January brought fresh baptisms of Pentecost, followed by the Welsh Revival and the Azusa Street Revival. This spread into the greatest healing wave of the 1940s and into the Charismatic Movement. The century ended in a massive movement of repentance in the Brownsville Revival in Pensacola, Florida. [5]

 Fireballs of glory, like the head of a comet, made war on the sin of their carnal flesh. As they were slain in the Spirit for days under *Oceans of Glory*, God pressed them to purity of heart.

God visits each century, at its onset, to give a witness of His glory to the generations living at the time. Those generations, in turn, will relay this witness of the goodness of the Lord to their children and to their children's children, as can be seen in the pattern of the patriarchs Abraham, Isaac and Jacob.

Harnessing the Wave

Those of the first generation experience the visitation fervently, receiving the commission to carry the torch to their children. If the children do not pick it up, then the third generation, near the end of a century, will be backslidden, reaping the fruit of the parents' sins and being judged.

The light of each revival is a precious treasure of brilliance given to illuminate the darkness of the unknown century that lies ahead. Revival is meant to inspire spirits, souls and minds, thereby influencing homes, churches and civil governments. They, in turn, were meant to reflect it, giving guidance, like the beams from a lighthouse, upon the dark and murky waters of lost humanity. The blazing light of revival reveals a path of escape from sin to liberty.

God's Word declares, *"Where the Spirit of the Lord is, there is liberty"* (2 Corinthians 3:17), but this must be responded to by an obedience to God's Word, which brings the wisdom to rebuild or revive. The word *revive* means "to bring to life again." Biblically, revival is the restoration of sacred foundations that have crumbled. Just as the prophets Nehemiah and Ezra rebuilt the walls of Jerusalem, we are to rebuild the Church with zeal and wisdom.

We encourage people to visit the revivals of our day, but if we only visit someone else's revival to experience the thrills for ourselves, with no concern for our own city, then we are selfish and not true carriers of that river. As one who carries water from a well, we must use a vessel (system or strategy) to pass the reviving waters on to others who are thirsty.

Comprehending the aim of the "flood," or the river of glory, will cause an awakening in our modern society among those who are very comfortable with their sin and have no taste for mention of any negatives — such as Hell. Harnessing that fear in unregenerate man, to turn him to repentance, with the anchor of hope in Christ and the bounty of His goodness, is the goal. A merciful God wants us to behold our sin so that we no longer continue to live in it, but, in repentance, may turn to receive the bounty of blessings in life that He offers. We must declare mercy and repentance before the holiness of grace can come in *Oceans of Glory.*

 We must declare mercy and repentance before the holiness of grace can come in *Oceans of Glory.*

Only a tidal-wave-sized move of the Spirit will cause men and women to respect the moral codes that change a population, emptying the prisons, pubs, whorehouses and other haunts of sin. Only to the depth of our repentance shall rise the height of revival.

Though the flood of God's glory may cover a city, signs and wonders alone will not revive a wayward generation — no matter how extreme the expression or the experiences. Unless sound biblical teaching accompanies the outpouring of such manifestations and balances the mind with the spirit, decadent, immoral thought patterns will dominate our lives. The unregenerate mind is like a damaged canal that leaks. If we are unable to channel the wave or harness the power of the resulting flood, many will only be washed onto dry land again. We desperately need the proper focus and goals in our prayer lives and in our pastoral care. God wants the flood of glory to bless us all.

 Only to the depth of our repentance shall rise the height of revival.

The early apostles of Pentecost's first *Oceans of Glory* wave were a well-prepared people. Though surprised, they were ready. They had just graduated from three years of intense ministry training with the Living Word, Jesus Himself.

The canals of their minds were cleansed and ready to channel the *Oceans of Glory* as a pure river flowing from the thrones of their hearts, where Jesus now reigned. *"The pure in heart ... shall see God"* (Matthew 5:8).

Pastor John Maher, of St. Mary's Episcopal Church in Elverson, Pennsylvania, told me this wonderful revelation: "While in Phoenix, I was riding my bicycle through the canal system in that city. At several points along the bike path there were signs that read 'FLASH FLOOD AREA.' The Lord spoke this to me: 'Build a system in the local church I have placed you over to hold what I am going to pour out. When it flows through the system, it will bring life. If it escapes from the system, it will bring destruction.' I went back to the church I have been pastoring intent on building a system that can hold what the Lord is ready to pour out."

On a tape widely circulated by the Brownsville Assembly of God in Pensacola, Florida, Evangelist Steven Hill made a significant statement that clarifies this thought. He said, "It doesn't matter how they fell in the prayer lines, but what did they do with the anointing when they got back up." In other words, are lives being changed through our ministries?

Even though we gratefully admire the large revivals of our time that have spanned many months continuously, we must understand that counting weeks in any local church is not necessarily the mark of being in revival.

Many, in copying what worked for others, have accomplished little more than wearing out their congregations, by straining to keep the church open nightly. If revival is not fueled by prayer, it will be a hollow "flash in the pan." With the help of modern technology, we compete with the world's advertising for the attention of the masses, but our striving to do so can sometimes be a means by which the devil wearies the saints.

The significant question is not "How many nights a week is your door open?" but rather "How many souls are saved? Are lives being truly changed for a healthy and prosperous future?" God has not called us to be echoes, but voices! We should each be seeking God for His unique plan for our individual cities. The sermons will be different, the music will be original, from the throne of God, and the manifestations will also be diverse.

God has not called us to be echoes, but voices! We should each be seeking God for His unique plan for our individual cities.

This true revival will not only include an awakening of epidemic proportions, but a sound reconstruction of moral and biblical character. It will be evident in all phases of society and government. The massive fortifications of sin must be matched by equal and greater force in order to approach the captives held within. An enemy is best attacked suddenly, and so the tsunami will come! Those who are tuned in to well-planned strategies of the Holy Spirit will preserve their cities afterwards and gather the spoils — an unprecedented harvest of souls!

A great reconstruction must come after the next tidal wave of God's glory, and it will. When the final wave hits the last generation, Jesus will greet the Church with a new heaven and a new earth prepared for those who are ready.

Jesus has been preparing us with Holy Ghost demonstrations at the close of this recent century. Concurrent with this era began the shakings of repentance in the late 1990s in Argentina, in Toronto, Canada, and in Pensacola, Florida, in America. God has once again been revisiting the patterns of massive revival. Now, He desires that our spirits and our minds be readied to receive not only the river, but the coming *Oceans of Glory.*

WAVES OF GLORIOUS EXPERIENCE

In spite of our theological objections, history recounts that all of the revivals — of 1601, 1701, 1801, 1901 and the late 1990s — commonly recorded many of the same manifestations of religious experience — barking, [6] jerking, dancing, bursts of running and speaking in tongues and the sudden appearance of angels, golden rain, or the supernatural sounds of heavenly choirs with instruments of music. [7]

During the First Great Awakening, Rev. Jonathan Edwards wrote: "A great joy came upon the people that caused them to laugh, shriek, shout, jerk and shake." His wife experienced "heavenly bliss" for seventeen days, fainting in the Spirit or being slain "by the exceeding power of His presence," which included trances and visits to Heaven. [8]

SEAWALLS OF RESISTANCE

All the revivals endured great persecution from the pens of heresy hunters and religious critics, who only saw them as an explosion of uncontrollable power, much like the wild arcing of electricity from a broken power line. But the revivals drew the curious lost, bringing many thousands within earshot of the salvation message and showering upon them the goodness of God in manifested healings, inspiring visions and ideals that even transformed governments. This cannot be discounted, and the pattern will repeat.

We must prepare for the tsunami with open hearts, avoiding a critical spirit. I myself had to repent of criticism after, having no firsthand knowledge of an event I had only read about, I spoke foolishly and publicly against one of the most unusual manifestations that some experienced in Toronto. It is better to say you know nothing than to repeat ignorance and insult the Holy Spirit. It turned out that my friend Dr. Shirley Elenbaas, president of White Horse School of Ministry in West Lafayette, Indiana, had been a participant in the thing I questioned.

 It is better to say you know nothing than to repeat ignorance.

As she explained the phenomenon, it made perfect sense. Such a flood of glory had suddenly come upon those who were praying that, in their joy to express it, they experienced expanding diaphragms, much like bellows, and could not breathe fast enough to express what they were feeling. While they desired to expel a fiery praise to God for such a mighty touch, it came out sounding similar to a cough or "bark" to many of those who were present. She said it sounded to her more like the sound seals make. As the people gasped for breath, great volumes of air passed over their vocal cords, and that air was pregnant with the weight of God's glory.

Though some others may only have imitated this manifestation, trying to be a part of the latest exciting phenomenon and thereby souring the moment, that does not discount the purity of the thing as Shirley described it. This was truly an unusual phenomenon, but should we be surprised? It is not new and has been reported in previous revivals.

After repenting of my criticism, I was in a church in Minneapolis where the glory fell so heavily in a prayer service that I, too, absolutely could not breathe. In the holy hush that followed, I gasped, but was not able to express any sound. This was the same Holy Spirit at work. In the Welsh Revival and at Azusa Street in the early 1900s, many of these same phenomena were also experienced.

FLOODWATERS OF CHANGE

When the *Oceans of Glory* from Heaven rest upon us, they are heavy, and their pressure changes human nature and events. The word *glory, kavod,* in Hebrew, also means "weight" or "wealth." *Oceans of Glory* contain resources, and God deposits them in moments like these. This may be seen in a series of events that changed the world in 1901.

Flames of revival in a modern-day Pentecost of tongues came to Topeka, Kansas (through Rev. Charles Parham), and then to Azusa Street in Los Angeles (to Rev. William Seymour), beginning on January 1, 1901. On a parallel track, the rebirth of the spoken Hebrew tongue (after its virtual disappearance for almost two thousand years) came in that same time frame through Eliazer Ben Yehuda to the Jews, God's first covenant people. Along with those two great spiritual events (and from yet another hidden well of reserve) came the gushers of Spindletop, the largest oil well in the world to that date, on January 10 of that same year, a joint venture of Gentile and Jewish geophysicists. As the "gushers" of glory were again filling empty, praying Gentile vessels with tongues of fire and Jews with biblical speech, Spindletop exploded with the wealth to spread the testimonies of revival as *Oceans of Glory* hovered to disperse it.

As the birth pangs of end-time wars, World Wars I and II, became more fierce, the revival increased in magnitude of matching and greater force. Pastor Bruce Parks of Nobleboro, Maine, recently took me to a revival spot in that state which he owns, where three thousand people traveled to a wilderness area at the end of the 1800s to participate in a campmeeting. They spoke in tongues and made intense intercessory prayer, even taking ocean journeys to the Ivory Coast of Africa to supplicate Heaven for the lost souls on "the dark continent" of their day, for nothing of lasting value is ever birthed into the Spirit realm without coming through the birth waters of the womb of prayer. Perhaps the modern-day Church owes a great debt to these obscure believers. Rev. Parham thought so, having traveled to Maine to interview them in December 1900, the last month of the nineteenth century. While absent from his Bible school in Topeka, Kansas, he left praying students on assignment to investigate Pentecost. In the first month of the twentieth century, he returned with a spark of Pentecostal fire, and his students received tongues. A torch had been passed from one century to another.

 Nothing of lasting value is ever birthed into the Spirit realm without coming through the birth waters of the womb of prayer.

Our knees are much too smooth — no calluses! Our churches are too often more like secular organizations than birthing rooms of prayer. We have programs and covered-dish suppers, workout rooms and pools. After we finish these activities, we sometimes quickly run through the prayer list before we all go home. But the Church of the Lord Jesus Christ is not an organization, but an organism. It was intended to be a spiritual womb, able to give birth to new converts through the labor of Holy Spirit-led prayer.

Travailing on the cross, Jesus birthed a Bride (the Church) from His side with covenant blood and water (both elements of natural birth). The atmosphere of sin must be ripped open. Of this birth water, Jesus spoke:

Oceans of Glory

"If anyone is thirsty, let him come to me and drink. Whoever believes in me, as the Scripture has said, streams of living water will flow from within him."   John 7:37-38, NIV

Our Spirit-led prayers can draw out the substance for the next revival from Heaven to earth, both spiritually and physically. The *Oceans of Glory* that are sweeping the world will contain a vast financial supply for birthing the end-time harvest, as that which gushed from Spindletop in the days of Azusa Street and the Welsh Revival. My friend Hayseed Stephens, president of Ness Energy, called me one day some months ago on my cell phone. At that moment, I was praying at the Methodist campmeeting tabernacle on Martha's Vineyard, commanding it to reopen its well of revival fervor. As I was speaking to its foundations (as Ezekiel spoke to the valley of dry bones), the call came. Could it be a coincidence that God Almighty chose the man who is digging the deepest oil well on earth (35,000 feet, at the base of the Dead Sea in Israel) to call me that exact day and at the exact moment I was speaking to the revival well to reopen in the realm of the Spirit?

Hayseed was calling to give me a good report. His drilling lease had been extended so that a larger drill bit could be constructed. When he drills that well, the cycle will be completed in synchronization with revival once again. Then the most massive movement of harvest that the world has ever seen can be financed through the deepest gusher in the world. (You can track the progress of the well with us at www.nessenergy.com, as we hope to watch the miracle happen.)

And I love this part: Hayseed has told me that when roughnecks hit oil, it is allowed to gush. They do not try to separate the mud and litter from the oil. They simply move out of the way and yell, "Let her rip!" When the cycle of revival returns on the next wave of ocean glory, like a comet with fireballs, the Church should do the same. Let's get out of the way, stand back and yell, "Let her rip!" As I shouted this in my sermon in Malaysia recently, people came up out of wheelchairs. "Let her rip!"

We have been yearning to see the motherlode of all waves return to its earthly shore from Heaven for two thousand years now. This is what we have all been waiting for. Miracles will abound, if we can just stand aside and enjoy the beauty of what God is doing, something far greater than crude oil pouring from the earth. If we will prepare ourselves in God's Word and possess biblical wisdom for this event, even as roughnecks carefully and skillfully prepare the drill site, then we can take a strong spiritual stance, with no fear of injury to ourselves or our disciples, and enjoy the exciting rewards! I want to be among those who are known as the "Openers of the Gate"! Let us be those who say, "Let the miracles flow!" "Let her rip!"

A merciful God longs to pour forth His mercy upon the hurting masses that desperately need His miracles. For the most part, they may remain ignorant of the intricacies of theological debate as to whether their miracles are from God or not. But they are not flocking to hear our discussions. Have you noticed?

Jesus said that healing is *"the children's bread,"* and He invites men and women to pull up to His table for a piping hot meal. It will happen when the fire and glory of God is allowed free rein. The late Raymon T. Richie called it "the dinner bell of healing." Through the demonstration of His power, God calls men and women to Himself, and He is about to demonstrate His power as never before in history. When He has finished, He will have turned the earth inside out and upside down, and we will never be the same again:

> *But the day of the Lord will come as a thief in the night; in the which the heavens shall pass away with a great noise, and the elements shall melt with fervent heat, the earth also and the works that are therein shall be burned up.*
>
> 2 Peter 3:10

Though the "laughing" and "shaking" revivals of the late 1990s were refreshing, their force has not yet brought full revival to all churches, nor to all of the highest government offices of our land. A great outpouring, the tsunami, must yet come!

ENDNOTES

1. Forerunners are already appearing as this book goes to press. In Oklahoma City, we met a woman who sang at TBN Channel 14 while we were hosting one day. She related the testimony of a bartender in the city who had been saved and turned the bar into a church. Then we saw a news clip of the man on the local news dumping out his liquor as the patrons were being saved one by one and joining him in the transformation of the bar into a church. Recently, in Calgary, Canada, a man publicly burned all his inventory for his pornographic store in front of television cameras. He was turning the building into a place to worship God.
2. This sermon is available in MP3 format at our website, www.harvestprojects.com. You may also request it by e-mail at harvestprojects@cfaith.com.
3. Charles E. Coffin, *Sweet Land of Liberty*, Maranatha Publishers (Gainesville, FL: 1992).
4. Please see my explanation of this phenomenon later in the chapter.
5. Trace the history of the Brownsville Revival in an account by Renee DeLoriea: *Portal in Pensacola*, Revival Press (Shippensburg, PA: 1997).
6. Ellen B. Weiss, *City in the Woods: The Life and Design of an American Camp Meeting on Martha's Vineyard*, Northeastern University Press (Boston: 1987).
7. Guy Chevreau, *Catch the Fire*, Harper Perennial Publishers (Toronto: 1994).

THE WINDS OF CHANGING SPIRITUAL CLIMATE

HE WAS SEEN UPON THE WINGS OF THE WIND. And he made darkness pavilions round about him, dark waters, and thick clouds of the skies. Through the brightness before him were coals of fire kindled. The LORD thundered from heaven, and the most High uttered his voice. And he sent out arrows, and scattered them; lightning, and discomfited them. And THE CHANNELS OF THE SEA APPEARED, the foundations of the world were discovered, at the rebuking of the LORD, at the blast of the breath of his nostrils. He sent from above, he took me; he drew me out of many waters.

2 Samuel 22:11-17

Early in 2000, I conversed by e-mail with my friend Dr. Flo Ellers of Global Glory Ministries in Juneau, Alaska. We were both excited about the wonderful creative miracles that had recently begun to appear in the meetings Ronnie and I were conducting. Flo felt that this rash of miracles was a sign that God was placing some forerunners prophetically into position, moving the envelope of time forward into the next century for a massive healing wave.

She reminded me that the great healing evangelist, Rev. Oral Roberts, and the younger prominent minister of the hour, Rev. Benny Hinn, had both recently prophesied on Trinity Broadcasting Network that a massive healing wave of glory was about to hit the Church once again, as it had in the early part of the twentieth century. Flo encouraged us to continue running with this blazing torch into our sphere of influence, igniting bonfires along the way. Soon, the entire Body of Christ will burst into flame in a full-fledged wave of healing miracles once again. Oh, the goodness and mercy of God! [1]

Ministering in long prayer lines with confidence and patience for creative miracles to replace missing parts was something new to Ronnie and me. We had read about such things and had seen the late Rev. Wallace Heflin, Jr., of Ashland, Virginia, and his uncle, Dr. William A. Ward (once the owner of the world's largest Gospel tent), perform this ministry with phenomenal results. But to enter into that course ourselves and not tire in the new pace was a whole new ball game. I appreciated Flo's encouragement.

Flo's fiery personality has been a light to our path since we met. A native American Indian, she has endured many trials for her people and has a backbone of iron. Our greeting to one another through the years has often been "You are fire that lights fire and iron that sharpens iron" (see Proverbs 27:17). She has often reminded me that neither of us can turn back on the revival trail we have blazed, because we could easily bump into someone else following hot on our heels. Everyone needs a friend like Flo Ellers.

 You are fire that lights fire and iron that sharpens iron!

It was Flo who, in 1998, introduced me to Dr. Nicholas Wu of Christian Life Center in Kuala Lumpur, Malaysia. This led to my taking many wonderful trips to visit Dr. Wu and his people, and I became intensely interested in their prophetic voice of prayer. They are a people on fire for God. I have found their faith to be unsurpassed. My experience with the zeal of the Asians has resulted in significant changes in my perspective on ministry and revival. The Christians of the Far East have a keen insight into the portals, or gates, of revival.

Our friend Linda Knight of Monroe, Washington, shared a prophecy from Dr. Tan Khian Seng of Singapore, who forecast that the winds of God will blow in a tsunami-sized healing wave and that many Christian leaders will think that the winds are of the devil and choose to fight them [2] (see Zechariah 6:5 and Revelation 7:1). This prophetic word from the East is significant in placing the changing climate of revival in perspective as we watch the storm brewing for a new downpour from Heaven. Jesus warned:

> *When it is evening, ye say, It will be fair weather: for the sky is red. And in the morning, It will be foul weather to-day: for the sky is red and lowering. O ye hypocrites, ye can discern the face of the sky; but can ye not discern the signs of the times?*   Matthew 16:2-3

The Bible reveals four of these winds:

- •A WIND of HOLINESS: like that of winter, which causes death to unfruitful branches and forces our roots, like those of trees, to burrow deep in the soil, taking us back to the basics of faith, awaiting spring rain. (See Job 37:9-10 and 21 — north wind that cleanses.)

- •A WIND of STRENGTH: joy in the refreshing of spring, new growth (see Job 37:17). *"The joy of the LORD is your strength"* (Nehemiah 8:10). (See Psalm 16:11 and Exodus 15:13 — south wind that warms.)
- •A WIND of the KINGDOM: spring buds turning to summer fruit. Prosperity in all things! Resources! (See Matthew 6:33 and Job 38:24-27 — east wind.)
- •A WIND of MIRACLES: autumn winds of judgment. Creative miracles of missing body parts, translations and the raising of the dead will come. But this will also signal danger for the hardened hearts of scoffers, who, even in that level of glory, continue to mock God (See Mark 6:25, Acts 19 and Acts 8:39 — west wind).

Jesus taught:

"The wind blows wherever it pleases. You hear its sound, but you cannot tell where it comes from or where it is going. So it is with everyone born of the Spirit."   John 3:8, NIV

Winds represent change. How can Christians believe that they are truly living the fullness of the born-again lifestyle when their schedules leave no room for change? What are revival people like? They will not be those who must punctuate the Sunday service with disgusted looks so that the preacher will dismiss them on time (to keep the roast from burning in the oven or the restaurants in town from filling up with people from other churches). Instead, they will be like those who, after being mightily touched by God at the turn of the twentieth century in Zion, Illinois, handed their keys to the ushers at the door, saying "Find a needy family to enjoy our house. I will be going to the mission field."

The testimony of John G. Lake was like that. He sold all that he had and put his fortune into the ministry. When he headed to a boat dock with his large family, he was without a cent left to pay for their steamer tickets. Cast upon the mercies of God, they prepared to travel "by faith" to Africa and launch the great church that raised up modern-day evangelist Dr. Rodney Howard-Browne and his brother Basil. (Returning to America on another wave, the Howard-Brownes also sacrificed.) At the ticket gate, a praying saint, who was alerted to the need of the Lake family by God alone, met them with the full fare for their tickets. John G. Lake had become Christ-like:

Jesus replied, "Foxes have holes and birds of the air have nests, but the Son of Man has no place to lay his head."   Luke 9:58, NIV

All four of these winds had blown on the John G. Lake family. The Wind of Holiness had taken pride out of them and caused them to redirect the purpose of the family fortune. The Wind of Strength replaced their sacrifices with joy. The Wind of the Kingdom blew in new resources, and the Wind of Miracles allowed them to change Africa. Let us each one cry in our hearts, "Oh, winds of God, blow on me! Blow through me! Move me!"

An e-mail message entitled "Suddenlies" by Rev. John Kilpatrick was forwarded to me. In it, he outlined spiritual changes he perceived to be blowing our way. Under the heading of "GOD'S STRANGE ACTS," he had this scripture that I find encouraging as I urge people to live outside their comfort zones:

> For the LORD shall rise up as in mount Perazim, he shall be wroth as in the valley of Gibeon, that he may do his work, his strange work; and bring to pass his act, his strange act. Now therefore be ye not mockers, lest your bands be made strong.
> Isaiah 28:21-22

The strange acts of God suddenly will move us into unusual circumstances like gusts of wind.

This message is mirrored in the words of a card I posted on my computer desk. It was from an assistant in our New England revival, Donna Nelson. The card reads "If you are not living on the edge, then you are taking up too much space." This constantly reminds me to press on when my flesh is weary.

My husband, Ronnie, listened to my exhortations in a meeting one night, and later he said to me, "Honey, I think we have preached ourselves right out of our comfort zone!" It was true. We had sold our home and offices a year before, in preparation for a massive move into a new headquarters in Branson, Missouri. Our household furniture was stored in the facilities of a board member in Tulsa, our office equipment in a mini-storage unit in Branson, and our fingertip items and suitcases in a cabin in Indiana.

Amazingly, as we traveled between locations, attending revival services in Indiana, conducting Sunday services in our new outreach church in Mansfield, Missouri, and preaching around the globe during the week, we were still able to write books, plan crusades and meet ourselves coming and going. What a stretch! But in traveling over a thousand miles a week for a year, we did reach many hungry people and bring in the harvest as we never had been able to do before. We followed the wind of God, not always knowing where and when it would take us.

You cannot reap if you fail to get moving to plow. Couch-potato Christianity will not work these days — even if the television is tuned to Christian programming all day long. As Jesus observed the harvest fields, He calculated the changing winds and understood that the harvest could not wait. He prayed for laborers for His fields. Who will set his or her sails and launch out into the deep with our Lord?

I love the painting by artist Stephen Sawyer of Jesus as the Captain of the ship, guiding it through the storms of life. (It can be seen at www.art4god.com/main.html.) Many, who have considered the voyages of the Spirit, have been faint of heart to begin, fearing the costs and risks involved. But Jesus did not commission us to venture forth alone or to end up shipwrecked. He is our great High Priest, interceding at the throne of God day and night for our success in harvesting souls. Even when He sent His disciples ahead of Him and they encountered a storm at sea, He cared for them in their trial:

> And straightway he constrained his disciples to get into the ship, and to go to the other side before unto Bethsaida, while he sent away the people. And when he had sent them away, he departed into a mountain to pray. And when even was come, the ship was in the midst of the sea, and he alone on the land.
>
> And he saw them toiling in rowing; for the WIND was contrary unto them: and about the fourth watch of the night he cometh unto them, walking upon the sea, and WOULD HAVE PASSED BY THEM. But when they saw him walking upon the sea, they supposed it had been a spirit, and cried out: for they all saw him, and were troubled. And immediately he talked with them, and saith unto them, Be of good cheer: it is I; be not afraid. And he went up unto them into the ship; and the wind ceased: and they were sore amazed in themselves beyond measure, and wondered. For they considered not the miracle of the loaves: for THEIR HEART WAS HARDENED.
>
> Mark 6:45-52

 He saw the disciples straining at the oars, because the wind was against them.

Jesus knew how to thwart winds of adversity that followed and buffeted His ministry; He always retreated to a solitary place to pray after performing great miracles. Perhaps such powerful ministry tired His body, but more likely, He wisely knew to refill His spirit man through direct contact with the Father in prayer. After our healing services, we try to do the same. This was the wise counsel relayed to us by a minister who knew of Oral Roberts' and Kenneth Hagin's habit of retreating to a private place in order to refill their own souls after their resources had been depleted in ministry. We were told that these men would spend time alone listening to the healing scripture promises on tape or reading and confessing them themselves.

When the anointing that brings miracles settles heavily upon a human body and moves through one's hands to others, there is often a draining effect after it lifts. It is wise to take much care to maintain the temple of the Holy Ghost with proper rest, diet and exercise. This helps to prevent burnout, which then leads to a hardness of heart and loss of godly perspective on the value of what was ministered.

Jesus was caught up in the spirit of prayer *"in the fourth watch of the night,"* and during His prayer, He could see His ministry team in trouble on the sea. This was an amazing miracle. I have been to Tiberius and Capernaum on the Sea of Galilee many times, and I can say that seeing as He did cannot normally be done.

I also saw for myself how dangerous the lake can be in a storm. The water is normally as still as glass, but once, in 1992, we were visiting there and saw how quickly that stillness can change.

Unusual spring rains broke a fifteen-year drought, so severe that it drew back the Galilee's shoreline until the exposed banks revealed an archeological treasure now known as "the Jesus boat." These rains also caused the seeds of blood-red poppies, hidden and dormant for thousands of years, to bloom in the desert around the Dead Sea. When our guide, Aaron Peak, saw this, he exclaimed, "My! My! My! Which of the prophets saw the wind of God hide the seeds of these poppies here in his day? Surely as he prophesied to the mountains to blossom in our day, he had no knowledge of how it would come to pass."

The statement thrilled my heart, for I realized that the latter rains of the Holy Spirit in the last-day harvest will also suddenly produce fruit in the lives of people who have been spiritual desert wastelands, void of any implication of interest in God. The seeds of many witnesses, through evangelistic crusades and media events, will suddenly respond. Overnight, the streamlets of people coming to Christ will become a river, and the rivers will converge into seas of new converts. Denominational barriers will be submerged in *Oceans of Glory*.

I was still thinking about this when we dined alongside the Sea of Galilee that night. Suddenly, as we discussed with our friends the wonder of what we had been seeing that day, the climate began to change. A howling wind began to blow, the sky turned black as night, and within a few minutes time, the sea was pitching in waves twenty feet high.

Concerned, we kept a wary eye on the scene outside our window, but we continued to eat. Suddenly, the waves washed over the boardwalk and hit the glass windows next to our table, flooding underneath to wet the carpet on the floor.

At this point, we Americans ran as fast as we could for the staircase. As we ran, our ears picked up a most unusual reaction from the native Israelis dining in the same restaurant. Amazingly, they were jubilant. *"Ness! Ness!"* they cried as they ran to the windows and pressed their noses to the glass, obviously fearing nothing.

"What are they saying?" we begged to know.

"Miracle! Miracle!" was the stunning reply. Sheepishly, we returned to our seats, finishing the meal. If the Jewish people considered the storm to be a miracle and were confident that the building would not be damaged, then we certainly did not want to be those *"of little faith."* The experience revealed how treacherous the sea was that had threatened the disciples lives. We also saw how unfamiliar winds can be misinterpreted.

After this, I tried to imagine Jesus praying upon the naked hillsides beyond our hotel. Those hillsides had not changed much since His day. No lights illuminated them. Even in the lights of the hotel below, I could never have seen a boatload of men struggling in the tempest of that storm. How could Jesus have seen the disciples in peril? He was miraculously caught up in the Spirit, and when He saw His disciples struggling, it was through the eye of the Spirit, not the eye of flesh.

I imagine Jesus, arising to answer their tortured cries. Walking in the glory, He never flinches as His feet leave the sandy shore and step upon the waves. A cushion of tangible glory is laid out before Him like a carpet. Following the urging of the Holy Spirit, He continues on in perfect peace. He does not even notice the waves.

But Peter did notice:

> *And when Peter was come down out of the ship, he walked on the water, to go to Jesus. But when he SAW THE WIND boisterous, he was afraid; and beginning to sink, he cried, saying, Lord, save me. And immediately Jesus stretched forth his hand, and caught him, and said unto him, O thou of little faith, wherefore didst thou doubt? AND WHEN THEY WERE COME INTO THE SHIP, THE WIND CEASED.* Matthew 14:29-32

Jesus would have passed the disciples by had they not cried out. How many times has God sent an answer to our situation, but we missed it because we did not turn to Him to receive it? The winds of the Spirit (and of the natural realm, as well) obey Him.

31

Oceans of Glory

When Peter asked Jesus to confirm that He was real, the Lord extended to him an offer to embark on the impossible with Him — a water walk. (He encourages us to test the spirits, whether they be of God or not.) How do you suppose Peter felt at that moment? Had not Jesus' instruction earlier in the day led him into this "mess" to begin with? Now, he was being asked to venture further into the deep to draw near to the Master. Do not expect the *Oceans of Glory* to bring tranquillity to your life, for they may not. They will challenge you to deeper waters. Jesus said:

> "Do not suppose that I have come to bring peace to the earth. I did not come to bring peace, but a sword. For I have come to turn 'a man against his father, a daughter against her mother, a daughter-in-law against her mother-in-law — a man's enemies will be the members of his own household.' Anyone who loves his father or mother more than me is not worthy of me; anyone who loves his son or daughter more than me is not worthy of me; and anyone who does not take his cross and follow me is not worthy of me. Whoever finds his life will lose it, and whoever loses his life for my sake will find it."
>
> Matthew 10:34-39, NIV

The first stages of entering the ocean are difficult, for we must bear the force of the crashing tides. But once a boat is well on its way, there are some moments of smooth sailing. It seems that we cannot find the peace of God or the eye of calm in the storms of life until we have ventured out, not only into the troubled waters, but then beyond that stage and into the very depths of them.

 Do not expect the *Oceans of Glory* to bring tranquillity to your life, for they will not. They will challenge you to deeper waters.

Would Peter not have expected Jesus to first calm the current tempest, return the boat to shore and apologize for sending them into the storm in the first place? Then, on a calm day, He could have invited them all to enjoy a delightful and amazing water walk? But it doesn't happen that way, does it?

Many are now embroiled in storms over the way the Holy Spirit has chosen to manifest Himself in their lives and ministries. Theologians have confronted them about the manifestations they are experiencing. Some church members have found themselves without churches, and some pastors have found themselves without congregations because others cannot understand their experiences.

Some have been anxiously awaiting the end of years of nightly revival meetings so that they and their families can "finally return to a normal life." Now, just when it seems that the river is receding, here come the waves of a new movement and the promise of even more radical change, *Oceans of Glory*. The winds are changing again. Jesus is not saying to us, "You can go back to shore now." No! He is calling, "Come! Walk on the water with Me!"

In 1979, I daily prayer-walked through my neighborhood in North Plymouth, Massachusetts, my trail invariably ending on a high bluff over the bay. I enjoyed the winds of change that always greeted me there, as the breeze and smell of the sea drifted up from the water. There, I could hide away with God, far from the hearing or sight of any person. Burying my face in the pine needles, I would pray about the course of my life and of that city. One day as I was praying thus, the Lord visited me in a vision. I saw the lightnings of God flashing across the eastern sky and heard the Lord calling, "Come, walk on the water to Me! Behold, I come quickly. Come, walk on the water to Me!" This I determined to do — even at the possible expense of career and family ties.

Years later, when my flesh and soul had wearied of the constant stretching required for water-walking with the Lord, I began to question every step, rebelling in heart. Isn't it amazing that, like the children of Israel, we so quickly forget the miracles of love and deliverance that God has poured out on us? He delivered the Israelites from Egypt, and yet they complained of eating manna. The disciples, because of the troubled boat ride that led to Peter's water-walking venture, hardened their hearts only a few short hours after watching Jesus feed the five thousand. This may be why only Peter walked on water and not the others. They were probably pulling on his coattails, urging, "Are you crazy? You will drown! As if we're not already in enough of a mess. Now you want to jump out of the boat and walk with Him?"

Jesus did not pull Peter into the water. The disciple would have to decide for himself. Of his own accord, Peter began to walk on the water toward Jesus.

No sooner had Peter begun to walk on water, however, than the wind and waves distracted him, and he began to sink. This is fairly typical of those who respond to the changing winds of spiritual climate. Many of those who joyously entered into the revival of the 1990s lost their joy quickly when their friends and loved ones complained about the unorthodox manifestations they saw. That was mild compared to what is coming. Will the faint of heart ever become successful water-walkers? Surely their hearts will first have to change, and they will have to become flexible to follow the changing winds of the Spirit.

As I cried out to God to release me from my water-walking lifestyle, He sent an unexpected answer. I was attending a service in 1986 at Lakewood Church in Houston, Texas, when the Lord began to show me the need of my soul. I was living in a stretched-out place, far from family, and I had become aware of not yet being in the exact destiny, or occupation, to which I had been called. Life was about to get even more strange, and all natural securities would soon be left behind on the shores of a place called "normal." And it would begin before I left the church that day.

At the close of the service, I was caught up so fully in worship that I could not seem to move out of the building with the crowd. I found my hands straight up in the air, stuck. *Oh, this is embarrassing!* I thought, *I've got to go, Lord! I've got to stop worshiping now. They are turning out the lights! I don't want anyone here to see me acting so foolish. What would people think?*

A wind of holiness answered me: "PRIDE!" It had to die. The fear of man versus the fear of God will shipwreck us. Only a few short years later, people everywhere were breaking out of the molds — laughing, dancing and shouting all night!

As I lingered, an elder of that church came by and grasped my outstretched hand. A Vietnamese cleaning lady also fell at my feet in hard travail of prayer. The two of them multiplied my embarrassment. But as they prayed, I saw a vision of Jesus calling me to walk on the water. I sensed Him saying, "Please, walk on the water a little longer. I need you to have this kind of faith."

I did not want to walk on water, but the Lord showed me a ship, a ministry that I would one day enter safely into. I said nothing.

About that time, the cleaning lady at my feet let out a wail that made me jump. Chiming in was the voice of the elder: "Ship ahoy! Ship ahoy! Ship ahoy! Walk a little longer. One day I will allow you to return to a safe shore, and then I shall call you yet again. Walk on the water to Me." I realized that the Lord had sent both of those individuals.

When the elder asked if what he had said meant anything to me, I could only laugh with relief. A wind of strength hit me. The joy of the Lord! It blessed the elder, who realized the prophecy was confirmed. He said it was the strangest prophecy he had ever uttered. God and I knew exactly what it meant. He is so good!

Though the wind be contrary to our flesh or even to God's chosen path for our lives, we must press through and set our sails to follow the course of a God-sent wind. Even as the Master of the winds caused them to obey Him and brought calm, He will govern the helms of our ships too — if we will let Him and do not quit.

The Lord of the Harvest would not send us to the other side unless there was a harvest to reap there. And even though we must pass through some storms at sea, He sends a wind of victory into our sails. We must only discern which way the wind is blowing to set our course correctly.

King David discerned the wind with an instrument of worship, his harp.

Rabbis say it hung in the trees where he encamped against his enemies. One night, during the season when no desert wind blows, a refreshing wind suddenly played heavenly music upon the quiet strings. David interpreted this as "Arise! The *Ruach Kodesh* (Holy Spirit, breath of God) is upon us to defeat our enemies." And they did.

We must recognize that the wind signifies change — great change. The times of the Lord are upon us, and we will soon see *Oceans of Glory* crashing upon every shore.

ENDNOTES

1. Rev. Ruth Ward Heflin once shared a cup of coffee with me on her divan as we discussed the wind of healing. She testified that in the 1940s, healing miracles were so prevalent in Pentecostal circles that receiving them was as easy as breathing. The atmosphere was pregnant with God's healing power.
2. From *"The Winds of God"* by Rev. (Dr.) Tan Khian Seng, Ph.D. in theology, founder and pastor of Harvest Community Fellowship of Singapore.

Catch the Vision

Words and Music by
Shelli Jones Baker

pipe flute — Keyboard special effects: foghorns, and violins.

Coda — piano

1. We must all be sail-ors sail-ing in the wind, off to new hor- i-zons be-

2. (See the bottom of page two for the second verse.)

yond the clouds so thin. There stands a man of wis-dom there. He

climbs in-to our boat. Then lift - ing up His hand He says, "Be-

Hold, my friends, what lies a-head, be-yond the o- ceans, be-yond your

pipe flute

dreams.

D.S. — piano

There's trea-sure there, more pure than gold, more val- u- able than

pipe flute

dia-monds sold, the nat- tions of the world, be-yond your dreams."

piano

Catch the vis-ion! Catch the vis-ion! Won't you sail there with me?

won't you sail_____ a- cross this sea?_____ For be-

yond the hor- i- zon, there are na-tions to reach, where My story's not told_____

_____ and the world, My friends, is grow-ing old. And the

world is grow-ing old. Catch the vis-ion! Catch the vis-ion! Won't you sail

pipe flute   D.C. al Coda

there with me?

piano

Catch the vis- ion.   Catch the vis- ion.

Second verse:
   Through storm and gale, we must prevail. Prepare to throw the line across the oceans, for this is harvest time! Jesus reveals His glory. Revival fills the earth. The nets we cast for souls of men are bursting with new birth, as He calls unto His Bride, "Leave the land. It's sinking sand. Don't capsize in your boat. But use your faith to walk with me. I am Zion's hope."

(Visit www.harvestprojects.com for a MP3 file sample.)

CYCLES OF GLORY: DEBORAH, THE BEE

"Remember therefore from where you have fallen; repent and do the first works, or else I will come to you quickly and remove your lampstand from its place — unless you repent."　　　　　　　　　　Revelation 2:5, NKJ

The echoes of history would be nothing but a glaring rumble of war and cataclysmic events if it were not for the cycles of refreshing revival waves that roll in upon each and every century to remind the world of God's peace, love, joy and hope for mankind.

The tides of the ocean are rhythmic and soothing to listen to as they roll in upon the shore, one wave in sync with another. I love to walk along the beach barefoot and just listen. An eternal song sounds in the pounding surf, repeating its endless echo for thousands of years. It all speaks of the grandeur and glory of God, revealing little of the men who have traversed its depths in seasons of peace and war. Studying the seasons teaches us to embrace the glory waves in their cycles and draws us back to our first love.

In the 1980s, I experienced my first glimpse of the cycles of God as a young (twenty-year-old) student, just awakening to vast realms of His glory. I moved to Tulsa, Oklahoma, and experienced the city aflame with God every night of the week. There were always churches hosting seminars with wonderful speakers, and house prayer meetings were the rage all over the city. Our Bible school even hosted a prayer and healing school.

Through the 1980s, the move of the glory in prayer and the Word was widespread, and its brightness attracted thousands to a revival of intercessory prayer. Prophets warned those in the pulpits to keep their lives clean and holy, so that the marvelous works of God could progress throughout the world. Christian television carried the meetings to all the globe.

We did not want a river; we were believing for an ocean. As my missionary friend Robin Stein once said, "A river is local, but an ocean is global."

By the summer of 1980, campmeetings in Tulsa Civic Center reached twenty-three thousand in attendance. By 1987, a Sunday-morning congregation of five thousand met in the Mabee Center at Oral Roberts University. People were nicknaming the city "Tulsa-rusalem," "Christian Mecca" and "the Buckle of the Bible Belt." Tulsa was in her glory.

But by 1988, sin, theological feuds and persecution had begun to extinguish the revival fires. Much of the gloryspout was capped. The blazing spiritual fires of our fervency in prayer cooled. Churches split. Pastors' hearts bled. Intercessory prayer teams fled underground, hiding from nervous clergy who no longer trusted them. The relationship between pastors and intercessory prayer teams suddenly resembled that of a husband and wife on the brink of divorce. The finger of blame smoked like a gun.

Many godly and wise sages — such as Carmen Goodwin, Jeannie Wilkerson, Lydia Berky, Phil Halverson, David du Plessis (Mr. Pentecost) and others who had led us and prophesied warnings to us — moved on to Heaven, their tasks on earth complete. They sailed away to Heaven's shore on the last wave of that glory cycle, and an era was over. We had followed like divers to the depths of the ocean, and been drawn into the bowels of prayer. But without them, many could not bear the pressures of those depths and sprang up to the surface of life again with lightness and frivolity.

 A river is local, but an ocean is global.

Where was the glory that had seemed to spin around us like a cocoon of protection and splendor for those few short years? Was it gone forever?

How had it come in the first place? And what would bring it back? During this dry season, the Holy Spirit gave me some answers in the midst of a personal tragedy.

In one of my 1988 services at a church in Mansfield, Missouri, the Holy Spirit gave me the name of a sinner in the service — Lisa. When I said that there was such a person in the audience needing urgently to give her heart to Jesus, no one came forward. The pressure built, and I risked looking like a fool, but the prompting to fish for her continued. At last, a teary-eyed and frail teenager stumbled to the platform, broken and repentant before the Lord. Lisa Hurst was seventeen, and that night she caught on fire for Jesus.

Lisa became a dear friend and disciple. She evangelized the town, signed up for my mission trip and prepared to enroll in the music department of Oral

Roberts University. She was a firebrand of unusual brilliance in the hand of God that year. But, alas, she was to be a runner in a very short race. Only a few months later, we heard the sirens rushing to the scene of Lisa's fatal car/train accident. I prayed, against all reason and hope, for a miracle to sustain her as she was rushed into surgery. But as I prayed, Heaven's gates seemed strangely barred, as if nothing would move them.

During the preceding years of the glorious move of God in Tulsa, I could not recall ever having lost such a crucial battle in prayer. But now I was shocked to discover that, in fact, the power and glory of God upon the movement had lifted. The season had changed; the spiritual atmosphere was no longer pregnant with the same sovereign levels of glory.

All the "right" scriptures flooded my mind to plead against her death toward the court room of Heaven. I could give mental assent to the idea of raising her up, but the power and the glory were not there. Moments later, we were informed of her death, and there was nothing more to do. It was a most lonely hour.

My partners in prayer, who had once seemed as numerous and powerful as the hairs of Samson's head, somehow could not be found that day. And it was only then, in those empty, helpless moments, that I realized that just as a young life had been snuffed out, our move of glory and its strength had indeed departed. The great revival of prayer of the 1980s had been aborted, largely because of doctrinal errors and emotional excesses, and many besides my friend would never reach their generation.

Revivalists must be massively supported in prayer. Too many have run their races nearly alone, with low funding and bare resources of personnel. Crowds feast at their tables on the meat of the Word, waiting for the desserts of miracles, and revere them, but few return to truly serve or pray.

How badly do we want revival? There is a price to pay. Not one revival has ever begun without a massive prayer movement, and all have ceased when prayer stopped. How can we dare to enter the expanse of an ocean without a proper vessel? We traverse the *Oceans of Glory* in an ark of prayer filled with praise and worship.

At the time of Lisa's death, I felt the midnight of the soul setting in upon me. I could not seem to pray.

 Not one revival has ever begun without a massive prayer movement, and all have ceased when prayer stopped.

Finally, a woman of prayer, seasoned in her mantle, insisted that we go to our prayer room at the church anyway. We determined to stay until we would touch the heart of God and receive some answers to the many questions on our shattered hearts.

God is still a rewarder of those who diligently seek Him. I forced my flesh to my knees and dug into a familiar position of prayer with tenacity. There we remained, wrestling with the barriers until the answer of God arrived.

It came in a vision of prayer that I did not, at first, understand. I saw a gold belt buckle, majestically carved with honeybees, like the seal of a king. Two female hands grasped it tightly as it moved rhythmically back and forth. The woman's stride was bold and purposeful, and her garments shimmered with light. Her stride ministered consistency and strength to my soul. She was stepping into the glory. The vision relieved my pain, but I lingered to understand it all.

A decade later, when introduced to Ruth Heflin, I was struck by her similarity to this unknown figure in my vision. Ruth often taught about the rhythms of the glory and sang about stepping into the glory.

Julie Christopher, a prayer partner of ours at the time, heard me tell my vision and remarked, "Deborah! The Bee! God showed you the judge of Israel. Research the symbolism."

Reviewing the story of Deborah in the book of Judges (chapters four and five) caused us to refocus on God's Word. Though seasons of revival and prayer come and go, His Word never changes. It is the consistent absolute that gives us strength. God's Word is the cornerstone of all prayers that reach Heaven and of the revivals that they bring. It endures forever:

> *But the word of the Lord endureth for ever.* 1 Peter 1:25

 God's Word is the cornerstone of all prayers that reach Heaven and of the revivals that they bring.

All evening I searched Deborah's story, but found no mention of a bee. That night, my sleep was not quiet. I tossed and turned, feeling that I should rise and pray. But that activity was blocked again by painful memories of a prayer failure in the case of my deceased friend. Finally, I dreamed a vivid dream. As you read about it, note the cycles and rhythms of the glory.

In the dream, I was organizing the minute details of my life as if in preparation for an honored guest. The guest then appeared, and it was an elder minister for whom I had once worked in Broken Arrow, Oklahoma, in the art department of his ministry.

Dreams are full of symbols. In this dream, the minister passed by the art table at which I was working, as I cleared the remaining clutter of unfinished projects away so that he would not see them. I watched as he went to a large drawing table and began to unwind scrolls. They contained plans on the drawing table of Heaven for the next revival. (Through prayer, we draw such plans and strategies for revival out of Heaven.)

In my dream, I heard the minister say, "When things in the spiritual realm line up, then things in the natural realm will too." Then, with his finger lifted in the air, he drew an invisible sphere, and a tiny comet of light materialized and orbited the sphere, and he concluded, "And when things in the natural realm line up, then things in the spiritual realm will too!"

After saying this, he traced his finger in the air again, creating a second sphere around the first. As before, a comet of light appeared and began to orbit in the same pattern. Both spheres clearly worked together in perfect balance and brilliance. It reminded me of the symbol for an atom.

Suddenly, this serious conversation, with all the flavor of Einstein, abruptly ended when a UPS man came to deliver a package. The minister received it with joy. As he opened the package, a curious multitude of sick folk came to the ministry desiring healing. He opened the package in the midst of them, and they were healed. A healing wave was coming!

 When things in the spiritual realm line up, then things in the natural realm will too. And when things in the natural realm line up, then things in the spiritual realm will too!

Awakening from the dream, I understood the formula of the glory. It was a harmony of two realms, one of a sovereign God, the other, of an obedient people. Prophetic events on God's sovereign calendar harmonize with prayer and cycles of revival.

Does prayer bring revival or do the changing winds of the Holy Spirit prevail on praying hearts to prepare their generation to receive what is on its way? The farmer does not plant his harvest in winter, as there is no indication that it is the proper time to do so. In spring, when the climate changes, he prepares for harvest by plowing and planting in the proper season.

Likewise, a sailor never heads out to sea when the tides are wrong. He waits for just the right hour to launch successfully. To launch prematurely would cause much needless toil to correct the mistake.

After waking from the dream, I quickly looked up the Hebrew word for Deborah in the concordance and found this definition: "Bee: 1. To move in orderly motions; 2. With systematic instincts." I realized in that moment that God was showing me some simple truths about His glory. I now understood how it comes and what causes it to linger or depart.

 "Bee: 1. To move in orderly motions; 2. With systematic instincts."

God is a God of total divine order. He is more scientific than science, and to Him there is no difference between the beginning of natural laws, like gravity, and of spiritual laws, like faith.

 Awakening from the dream, I understood the formula of the glory. It was a harmony of two realms, one of a sovereign God, the other, of an obedient people. Prophetic events on God's sovereign calendar harmonize with prayer and cycles of revival.

Just as a break in a wire causes the flow of electrical power to cease, so a violation of spiritual law (such as sin or slothful living) causes God's glory to depart. We have not sufficiently respected this truth.

"Line upon line and precept upon precept," the Word of God lays out for us a plan. No one who is lazy about the Word of God will walk in the glory — in step, in tune, in time and in sync with the God of revival.

For the past twenty years now, the Holy Spirit has continued to teach us that faith and the integrity of God's Word are the foundation stones for stepping consistently into the next wave of glory. Go deeper!

Upon seeing the preview of the cover for this book, our friend Mark Summers had the following vision: "I saw the river and many people in it. Most were enjoying, but resisting, the flow of the tide out to sea. Those who did release the boundaries of the river were swept out to sea to the greater depths of the *Oceans of Glory.*

"In the depths, I saw these believers drawn down as the old World War II submarines used to dive to what were called then 'the sounding depths.' There, they determined the depth, their location and the location of the enemy. They also encountered the incredible pressure of the *Oceans of Glory.* Most stayed, but some chose to float free and escape, only to encounter the enemy on the surface.

"At those depths, one could escape the attack (depth charges) of the enemy. There were two choices the commander could make: (1) Dive deeper and encounter greater pressure (by which character is molded into Christ's image), or (2) Shut down the engines and all operations, commanding everyone on board to be still while the enemy was directly overhead. In this way, the submarine and its occupants remained hidden, even though the enemy was hovering in attack formation just above them.

"We must learn not only to be swept into God's *Oceans of Glory* and its depths, but we must learn to be still under the greatest pressures we encounter. In this way, God hides us from the fierce attacks of the enemy, even if he is directly above us. Go deeper in the *Oceans of Glory*, ever deeper."

No great sense of emptiness is felt in pausing to fill the fuel tanks of a speedboat, but oh, how overwhelming the sight of the gigantic empty tanks of an ocean liner. Great patience is required to prepare the greater vessel for a longer, deeper journey. Knowing that preparation time is never lost time, it is necessary if we are to be in position for the next revival.

Our accountability must be at the ultimate level, and any weaknesses of the flesh must be brought under control by developing the fruit of the Spirit and a consistent prayer life. Our feet must be untangled from the natural affairs of life as good foot soldiers in the army of the Lord. Then we will step in tune to the glory, and our song, like Deborah's, will be of victory (see Judges 5).

We would be mistaken to think that the glimpses of glory in past revivals came sporadically, with no discernible pattern, and could be played with irresponsibly. Instead, it has been the mercy of God to let us see His glory, and He will remove it again unless sin be consumed in us.

In this light, I came to understand Lisa's death. Though she is with Jesus, her life and its purpose were snuffed out prematurely, because her youthful steps were out of line with common sense criteria evident at the scene of the accident (in regards to the speed her friend was driving and other contributing circumstances). This happened in an hour when the evil one was seeking whom he might devour. He was especially delighted to eliminate someone who was winning souls. And when I could have been praying for her, I and others were preoccupied with the complicated daily schedules of life.

Like Deborah's symbol of the bee, we must keep our spiritual antennas up, stay in sync with the rhythms of glory in those heavenly ocean waves and be aware of their cause and effect upon earth around us. Never be too busy! Take no spiritual or earthly happening lightly. The enemy doesn't. Heavenly and earthly realms work together, and we must be soberly watching in prayer. Ronnie and I still praise God for a friend who *"watched"* for us.

At 6 o'clock one morning, Pastor Jan Morgans, of Collinsville, Oklahoma, called and woke us up. She said, "Whatever you do today, don't go out of the house without prayer, and avoid any strife." In all the years that we had known her, she had never told us such a thing before. But this was from God.

We prayed, and Ronnie left to renew our vehicle tags. I was to have accompanied him, but felt uneasy and decided to stay and pray longer. It was God's leading that I was not in the passenger seat of the van that day.

Not long after Ronnie left, the uneasiness gripped me further, and I knew that the trouble Jan had sensed had not been prayed through by our simple prayers of agreement and our pleading of the blood of Jesus. For whatever reason, some additional depth of prayer was required.

Sensing that I needed a heavyweight in the arena with me, I called Rachel Teafatiller, a closet "pray-er." I had never bothered her before, as I highly respected her daily work of hiding away in God to pray for many ministries and important assignments, but this was serious.

Rachel was delighted to receive my call, and we teamed up together on the phone in intense prayer in the Spirit. After a while, the burden lifted completely, and we began to laugh. We had a definite note of victory!

About 1:00 that afternoon, Ronnie returned with this news: He had been in an accident. Driving around a hairpin turn on a wet road, he had come upon a stalled vehicle. There was no time to stop and nowhere to go to get around the other vehicle. He slammed into the back of it, with violent impact and noise. Everything that had been loaded into the van (behind the passenger's seat, where I would have been riding), came crashing forward onto the dashboard.

When Ronnie got out to inspect the van, he was surprised to find no permanent damage. In fact, the only visible sign of the impact was in the front bumper (which had been bent in an earlier incident, when I left the van out of gear). Now, it was straightened and looked as good as new.

The lady in the other vehicle was fine. Before she got out, she shouted to Ronnie from the car, "Agree with me, in the name of Jesus, that everything is okay!"

Neighbors, who had heard the noise of the impact, came running to help and were shocked to note that there was no damage whatsoever. One bystander was so "freaked out" by this that he ran off saying, "This is too weird, man!"

God is good. I am so glad we were all "in sync" with the Holy Spirit that day, not just Ronnie and I, but also Jan and Rachel. Our obedience brought God's glory onto the scene.

Another incident in which people were marching "in sync" with a buckle of the glory of God comes to mind. In 1987, I had just returned from Russia with my boss's wife, Carolyn. While Carolyn unpacked her suitcases, I took their young daughter, Ruth Ann, out to get donuts for the office. On the way home, she began to sing a little jingle, "Ruiz, Ruiz, Ruiz." Then, she paused and asked, "What does it mean?"

I had no idea, but I humored her with possible explanations. What she was singing reminded me of the word *red* in Russian, and I wondered if she might have heard us say something like that, but she said she hadn't.

When we got back to the office, everything was in a flutter. Carolyn was weeping. She had just received a call from Brenda Steen, a friend of ours, asking us to pray for Brenda's sister, Chia Ruiz.

"Ruiz!" Even a child, in her naive and pure heart, could pick up on the rhythms of God's glory. Ruth Ann certainly had that day. She was far ahead of the rest of us. Her antenna was up.

I kept the children, and Carolyn flew out to Thousand Oaks, California, with other intercessors, who joined together on projects like this from time to time. They were a company. Their mouths and footsteps worked in perfect stride together like an army, and the enemy feared them. The early Church had powerful men and women of prayer like these known as companies:

> *And being let go, they went to their own company, and reported all that the chief priests and elders had said unto them. And when they heard that, they lifted up their voice to God with one accord.*
>
> *And when they had prayed, the place was shaken where they were assembled together; and they were all filled with the Holy Ghost, and they spake the word of God with boldness. And the multitude of them that believed were of one heart and of one soul.*   Acts 4:23-24 and 31-32

Chia Ruiz had given birth to her first child through C-section, and had suffered the backwashing of the amniotic fluid up into her bloodstream.[1] She hemorrhaged and clotted in several major organs simultaneously, which made medical help impossible. Doctors gave her up to die, but Brenda refused to do likewise. She flew into action at her sister's side like a general, and she called in reinforcements.

For two months, around the clock, this prayer battle and the battalion that waged it amazed Chia's doctors. Thirty intercessors stayed on the case around the clock in changing shifts. The parting charge to each shift was: "Don't let her die on your shift!" This was not a battle for the fainthearted. On every inbound and outbound tide, someone was praying, drawing deep drafts of the *Oceans of Glory* onto the scene.

Brenda told me that she used this scripture from Isaiah:

> *Thus saith the LORD, the Holy One of Israel, and his Maker, Ask me of things to come concerning my sons, and concerning the work of my hands command ye me.*   Isaiah 45:11

Although they prayed all the clots and hemorrhages away, Chia was brain-dead and unresponsive. One morning, a nurse came to check Chia, and she saw that all was as it had been the day before and many days before that. To the naked eye, it was an apparently hopeless case. But something *was* different that morning. There had been a stirring in the heavens.

Sometimes we pray too quickly for great miracles without the unction, and we frustrate the grace of God and cause people to give up. But Brenda and the team waited until the impossible void had been filled with prayers of faith and was overflowing with the requested miracle. On that morning, July 5, 1987, the Holy Spirit told Brenda to call a well-known prophet from Tulsa, Oklahoma. He had just received a word from God on Chia's condition before he got the call. They agreed together that it was time to wake Shia up. [2]

 The team waited until the impossible void had been filled with prayers of faith and was overflowing with the requested miracle.

The phone was put to her ear, and he said, "Chia, on the authority of God's Word, arise!" At that moment, Chia awoke from the coma and smiled! Soon afterward, she began singing this song: "Jesus is coming; you'd better get ready!" An awesome miracle had happened because a company worked together in the timing of God.

The prayer of a righteous man is powerful and effective.

James 5:16, NIV

Brenda sent me a copy of Chia's medical file, and I read it. It had been an impossible case, according to every doctor's report. But because an army of united, praying warriors, joined together in the systematic and orderly motions of God, continued to intercede around the clock for two months, she is alive and awake today. If for no other reason, God raised her up to be a testimony of His glory.

Buckle up with the belt of the bee. Led by the Spirit, in systematic instincts and orderly motions, we will fly like the bee into our battles, and we can expect swift and sure victories.

Scientifically, the bumblebee should not be able to fly, but he does. In the glory, we, too, will do the impossible in the days ahead. We will not only wade through challenging currents of rushing rivers, but we will traverse the impassable width of oceans.

ENDNOTES

1. You may read the amazing doctor's report on our webstie at www.harvestprojects.com.
2. See the article in *Word of Faith* magazine, January 1988, p.10.

SHAMAYIM: THE HEADWATERS OF HEAVEN

In the beginning God created the heaven and the earth. And the earth
was without form, and void; and darkness was upon the face of the deep. And
the Spirit of God moved upon the face of the waters.   Genesis 1:1-3

B°ree'shiyt	baaraa'	'Elohiym	'eet	hashaamayim	w°'eet	haa'aarets
בְּרֵאשִׁית	בָּרָא	אֱלֹהִים	אֵת	הַשָּׁמַיִם	וְאֵת	הָאָרֶץ׃
7225	1254	430	853	8064	853	776
In the beginning	created	God		the heaven	and	the earth.

Inerlinear Transliterated Bible copyright © 1994 by Biblesoft

Ha Shá/ma/yím is a Hebrew term that represents God's *Oceans of Glory*, not a
river or endless stream, but a vast eternal arena, of which there is no possible
sounding of its depths, nor ending to its boundaries. *"Deep calleth unto deep"*
(Psalm 42:7). God's *Oceans of Glory* are forever before, now and beyond all ages.

The *Ha Shamayim* are *"the heavens"* that God created, part of the celestial
sphere in which celestial bodies exist and rotate and from which they proceed
in degrees of God's tangible presence. Both Paul and John alluded to the higher
realms, or layers, of Heaven, for instance, when Paul mentioned *"the third*
heaven" (2 Corinthians 12:2).

This ancient concept has been traditionally taught by the rabbis from the Talmud. The Jewish *tallit*, or prayer shawl, is woven with seven deep blue stripes to
encourage the person praying to press in to and ascend in his prayers all the
way to the seventh, or highest, layer of Heaven. Moses did this when he insisted
that God not only reveal Himself in a burning bush and in the miracles of the
Exodus, the cloud and the fire on Mount Sinai (where the Law was given), but

also in a face-to-face audience. The cry of the heart of Moses was, "Show me Your glory," (or "More, Lord! More!")

> *Then Moses said, "Now show me your glory."*   Exodus 33:18, NIV

Joshua, Moses' scribe (who also spent forty days and nights on the mountain in a fast to record all that was given to Moses, and who also saw the same miracles), pressed in even further. In the tent of meeting, he surpassed his predecessor's quest and stayed longer in the glory:

> *And the LORD spake unto Moses face to face, as a man speaketh unto his friend. And he turned again into the camp: but his servant Joshua, the son of Nun, a young man, departed not out of the tabernacle.*   Exodus 33:11

It was Joshua who, greatly endowed with anointing and insight, led the Israelites forward into the Promised Land. If we are to go further in this final move of God, into the Rapture of glory, then we must be a people who will exceed our predecessors in our spiritual quests. We have far to go, for some of those who preceded us ventured much beyond anything we have yet experienced.

I feel so sorry for people who are bored with church and bored with God. Religion causes that. It is like living in a fishbowl or in the window of an aquarium next to the ocean. Fulfill your longings. Jump out of the container and go free! *Deep calleth unto deep!*

There is always a greater depth in the *Oceans of Glory* to explore. The possibilities are limitless. Joshua lingered in God's presence to find a greater depth, and Jesus did too. If we hope to reach the depths of such a place in God, we, too, must stay before Him longer when He manifests His presence tangibly. We must show Him reverence and push everything else aside for the joy of being in His presence. I never answer phones or doorbells when I have purposefully set time aside to seek the Lord and have invited Him to be my honored Guest. Would I interrupt an audience with an earthly king for a phone solicitor? How absurd! So, should we treat our Lord with any less respect?

When such moments of intimacy with the Lord come, let nothing disturb your peace, your *shalom*, your completeness in Him. This must become our goal in every hour of life, whether we are in the midst of a crowd or in the solitude of our prayer chambers. Jesus walked in this way, conscious of earth, but also lingering in the obedience of a heavenly call to continuously fellowship with God. Paul, too, learned to *"pray without ceasing,"* thus living in two realms at once.

Fulfill your longings. Jump out of the container and go free!

The nature of the Holy Spirit is to "hover," or "brood," or "meditate," in the *Ha Shamayim* of Heaven and over the waters of earth before He moves into action. He woos us to linger and wait with Him (see Genesis 1:1-3). Jesus particularly gave us an example by His willingness to linger in the presence of the Father. When Lazarus lay ill and dying, Jesus continued to linger. Even after Lazarus died and his body began rotting, Jesus lingered.

Lingering in the presence of the Father had long been Jesus' habit. When He was still young, Mary and Joseph began to journey home from their visit to Jerusalem, but Jesus lingered with the doctors of the Law in the Temple. He was on heavenly business and could not be rushed. Mary and Joseph left for home, but Jesus stayed behind, eventually requiring their return to search for Him. God's plan abruptly altered the schedule of Joseph and Mary.

Jesus' disciples were drowning in a boat on the Sea of Galilee, but He lingered on, praying *"in the fourth watch of the night."* His chosen men were going down fast, but He chose to linger in prayer. At last, He arose and walked on the water to them, saving them just in time. He had been secure all along in the presence of His Father.

Had the disciples not cried out to Jesus, *"He would have passed them by."* He was walking in the anointing for whoever could take hold of it. For those who could not, He remained in the anointing and would not make an exit to step into their turmoil. Only in the anointing did deliverance exist. The *Shamayim* of Heaven is an eternal river of joy and an ocean of peace.

One day, toward the beginning of Jesus' ministry, His family called Him home. He chose, instead, to linger with a crowd of worshipers and explained that His family consisted of those who loved and sought His Father. Jesus lingered in His heavenly Father's presence.

Jairus, an important man, needed Jesus to heal his daughter, but on the way that day there was a woman with an issue of blood who might have had more faith than Jairus. Because of that woman, Jesus lingered there. This divine delay only served to elevate Jairus' faith, and he too received his miracle.

Poverty cried out, but Jesus lingered long enough to allow a woman to expend all her wealth (contained in a single alabaster box) upon His feet. When He was told that there were many poor people who needed His attention, He responded that they could wait. *"You have the poor with you always,"* He explained to an angry and confused audience. He remained focused.

A Pharisee was waiting for Him, but Jesus lingered.

Martha and Mary invited Jesus for dinner. Food needed to be cooked, but the very astute Mary lingered at the feet of Jesus, and He encouraged her to do it.

We must learn to linger at altars of prayer when the anointing comes. There could be no more precious place. All else can wait — even some "crisis."

I am ever more amazed at those who tell me that they cannot invest an hour of their day in rehearsing God's healing promises, yet end up terminally ill, wasting weeks of life, in debt, in hospitals and doctors' offices, with no time for Doctor Jesus. Be caught away, lost at sea! Linger in God's *Oceans of Glory*. You can't afford not to. Therein is the answer to your problem.

To "swim" in the oceans of Heaven (*Ha Shamayim*) is to pray. I often observe congregations worshiping when I go out to preach. Many of them know a popular song about "swimming in the river of God," but some do not seem to have a clue about what they are singing. They are able to dance or panto-mime the action of swimming, but then they fail to pray and linger at the altars.

 Jesus lingered in His heavenly Father's presence.

One of my favorite heroes of prayer was the early twentieth-century pioneer circuit-riding preacher C.G. Bevington. [1] He founded churches in Gospel-resis-tant areas of America with no other tool but prayer. Often sleeping in a barn loft, haystack, hollow log or other such accommodation, his constant quest was prayer that reached the throne, affecting earth. He learned the secret of lin-gering before the Lord.

Once, a group of poor people had rented a boarded-up schoolhouse under much resistance and persecution from the neighboring community so that Bevington could hold a revival and lay the foundation of a church. Their emo-tions must have been very tender. Still, on the opening night, when Bevington arrived to preach, he perceived that the building was in fine shape, but the people were not ready in spirit. In their busyness, none of them had prayed through. He announced that revival was prayer, finding an audience with God. Then he made a quick exodus from the shocked crowd and climbed a ladder to the attic, where he stayed, praying for hours, ignoring demands that he descend and begin the service immediately.

Finally, when he heard the people begin to pray, he slipped out another way and did not return until the next night. When he arrived the next night, he found a curious crowd gathered, but still he repeated his performance of the night before. He did this for several more evenings, until he finally entered a building full of travailing people who had poured their souls out to God for re-vival instead of looking for entertaining words from him. A great revival ensued, and the result was a vibrant church. The fountains of the deep inside of those praying vessels brought forth "gushers" of glory.

When our prayer meetings exceed the attendance of our Sunday morning services, then we will know that we are truly revived. When more of our people have a burning desire to talk with Jesus, revival will be here.

We cannot attempt to "tweak" this revival under pressure from those who simply love the spectacular. We cannot midwife the move of God into existence prematurely. It will be born of the Spirit when it is born. To manufacture revival to please those around us and to appease our consciences into thinking that all is well may be the constant pressure from the church world. But bringing in *Oceans of Glory* will require days of "carpet duty" — intense prayer — on our part.

 When our prayer meetings exceed the attendance of Sunday morning services, then we will know that we are truly revived.

No one has gone this far before, to the very end of the age. This is the last move that will carry us across the divide of earthly and heavenly realms, to Heaven's happy shore. This is the last day, and it will have all of its own surprises. Some uncharted waters yet await us. We must salute the Holy Spirit and surrender to His control in obedience: "Aye, aye, Sir! Fill up the sails. We are homeward bound, heading out to sea ... into deep water."

Mayim is a Hebrew root word that means "water." It forms part of the word for Heaven, *Ha Shamayim*, in Genesis 1:1 and in Jeremiah 10:13. The most basic sense of this word is obvious. It represents the fluids of life. I see this as an indication that the heavens are a type and shadow of liquid, or fluid, the eternally running headwaters of God. *Ha Shamayim*, "Heaven," is the fountain of God, the fountains of the deep, an ocean source with no beginning or end. It is made up of liquid glory fires.

It is true that God created an actual first heaven of physical substance that included seven original layers of firmament. One fell in Noah's flood and dramatically altered the infrared levels of the sun's rays upon the planet. Scientists tell us today that our own environmental sins, since Adam stopped "keeping" the garden or planet, have severely eroded another layer, the ozone. However, just as Paul taught that there were layers of heaven (in agreement with the Talmud and rabbinical teachings), it is scriptural to recognize that those seven physical layers are only a mirror of what lies hidden in the spiritual layers and limitless expanse of eternity beyond the veil.

Water has always been an expression that is tightly connected with the symbolism of the Holy Spirit. It appears in relation to both Old and New Testament laws, events, visions and dreams.

A dream about water once beckoned me to the side of a sinner in need. She was suffering from insomnia due to a troubling and recurring dream. It was not a nightmare, but it was a puzzle that haunted her — even in her waking hours. Night after night, she dreamed that she stood at the edge of an Olympic-sized swimming pool, desiring to plunge in, but unsure of what would happen if she did. She was not a good swimmer.

I knew exactly what the dream meant. "You need the Holy Ghost!" I told her. Then I explained the symbolism of the Spirit as water in the Bible and "swimming" as prayer. She prayed with me on the spot and received the Lord and the power of His Spirit right there. God had been trying to bring her into the refreshment of His presence for months.

 Water has always been an expression that is tightly connected with the symbolism of the Holy Spirit.

We first meet the Holy Spirit in the Bible (see Genesis 1:2) as He is brooding, or thinking, over the puzzling waters, or depths, of chaos. In the New Testament, Jesus had His first public audience with the Holy Spirit in water at the banks of the Jordan, as He was being baptized by John. There are many other instances in the Bible where God associated His character with the symbol of water. Here are a few:

- The Israelites met the delivering hand of God in water as He parted the Red Sea.
- Jesus walked on water and also turned water into wine. He asks that all converts be baptized in water as a symbol of entering the depths of God, drowning our old, sinful natures.
- The first substance that God created on earth was water. Water issued forth from Eden in four rivers. (I heard Sister Glenyce Doorn of Florida teach a wonderful sermon on their significance: a river of *purity* (holiness), a river of *peace* (strength), a river of *prosperity* (Kingdom) and a river of *power* (miracles). These are the waters of revival, just as there are four winds.

A river watering the garden flowed from Eden; from there it was separated into four headwaters. Genesis 2:10, NIV

 A river of *purity* (holiness), a river of *peace* (strength), a river of *prosperity* (Kingdom) and a river of *power* (miracles). These are the waters of revival, just as there are four winds.

- A miracle river will flow from the Temple Mount in Jerusalem to greet the Messiah, Jesus (*Yeshua* or *Hashem* in Hebrew). It will flow all the way to the Dead Sea (see Ezekiel 47:1-11).

In the early summer of 1999, a news article from Israel appeared stating that water had begun to seep uncontrollably into the Temple Mount under the Dome of the Rock. According to the article, so great had been the seepage that some frustrated religious pilgrims had to take up their prayer mats, wringing wet with water. Some sources stoutly denied the report, but whether it be true or false, there will come such a day.

- In the center of spiritual Heaven, there is a river that comes from the very throne of God:

And he shewed me a pure river of water of life, clear as crystal, proceeding out of the throne of God and of the Lamb.　　　　　Revelation 22:1

- The voice of God, full of glory, sounds like water:

And, behold, the glory of the God of Israel came from the way of the east: and his voice was like a noise of many waters: and the earth shined with his glory.　　　　　Ezekiel 43:2

- Salvation in Jesus flows as water from a fountain that did not begin with the blood at Calvary, but in the liquid glory of eternity past. God portrays Himself as the Fountain of eternal life.

For my people have committed two evils; they have forsaken me the fountain of living waters, and hewed them out cisterns, broken cisterns, that can hold no water.　　　　　Jeremiah 2:13

O Lord, the hope of Israel, all that forsake thee shall be ashamed, and they that depart from me shall be written in the earth, because they have forsaken the Lord, the fountain of living waters.　　　　　Jeremiah 17:13

The *Oceans of Glory*, a vast and eternal supply, are only withheld from us by our inability to contain them. Elisha told a widow in need of a financial miracle to collect empty jars, even to boldly require them of her curious neighbors. He admonished her, *"Borrow not a few"* (2 Kings 4:3-7). Then, God sent a supernatural flow of oil that stopped only at the brim of her last container. It was not God who held back the supply, but simply the lack of another empty vessel to fill. To have a great revival, keep bringing the lost.

My friend and mentor, Rev. Billye Brim of Prayer Mountain in Branson, Missouri, illuminates this spiritual principle in her teachings on the goodness of God: 'God is good all the time' is a popular Charismatic phrase, but actually it is superseded by the truth of 2 Chronicles 5:13. Time is a limited part of the history of eternity, but God is actually good forever – beyond time. One day 'time' will be no more, but God shall continue to be good with full and overflowing supply." [2]

Billye Brim introduced me to the writings of David Baron, a Jewish scholar: "Goodness is very frequently attributed to God. Goodness is that attribute of God whereby He loveth to communicate to all who can or will receive it; all good, yea, Himself, who is the fullness, and universality of good, creator of good, this good, His goodness bestoweth on all and each to the capacity of each to receive it, nor is there any limit to His giving, only the creature's capacity of receiving, and that also is a good gift from Him." [3]

Billye also reminded me of the insights which I had read by the evangelist F.F. Bosworth in his book *Christ, the Healer*. He said: "Benevolence is the great attribute of God. Therefore if you want to please Him, remove the obstacles out of the way of the exercising of His benevolence. He is infinitely good, and He exists forever in a state of entire consecration to pour forth blessings upon His creatures, whenever they make it possible, which all may do. Suppose the vast Pacific Ocean were elevated high above, then conceive of its pressure into every crevice, seeking an outlet through which it may pour its ocean tides over all the earth and you will have a picture of God's benevolent attitude." [4]

It is ridiculous to argue over the measure of what God can give to you so that you can serve Him. He wishes for us to have giant faith levels to become storehouses for the *Oceans of Glory* to fill and thereby be dispensers of great wealth to accomplish all the word of the Gospel and bring in a great harvest of souls.

How do we get that great ocean power within our lives? We must dissolve the barriers in our thinking to experiencing the limitless depths of God. The locks are best removed from the floodgates of our lives by receiving the permission of the Word of God to open them. Study about the goodness of God and His desire to release it through praise, prayer and disciplined speech.

How do we access the *Oceans of Glory, Shamayim*? The same way God brought them into existence in the first place — through words — "Light be!"

The Hebrew word *dabar* is defined as "thing," "word" or "speech." By praise, prayer and the power of the Word of God, spoken into our world, we create a container of things for God to fill with *Oceans of Glory*. He is waiting for our utterance of faith to unlock the floodgates in our lives.

In John 4, Jesus expressed to a woman He encountered at a well in Samaria that He had a vast supply of water that superseded the depth of the well from which she had come to draw. That was remarkable, because that particular well was known as Jacob's Well and had been, from ancient times, one of the deepest in the Holy Land. As Jacob had come and reopened the well of his forefather Abraham, so Jesus, of that same lineage, had come to sample a refreshing, reviving drink from the ancient source.

Jesus had a right to that well (and He has a right to revisit His revival wells too, churches that once knew Him), but He had no dipper in Samaria. Therefore, He asked the Samaritan woman to draw water for Him.

Jesus did not so much want the lady to draw water as to catch a revelation that she was to be a bearer of the water that would always revive. He is visiting us through His Holy Spirit in this hour, to seek those who will draw water out of the vast supply of His glory, His oceans that never run dry. He is seeking those who will gladly reopen the ancient wells of revival and give a thirsty world something eternal to drink. But whom will He choose? You may be surprised.

 He is seeking those who will gladly reopen the ancient wells of revival and give a thirsty world something eternal to drink. But whom will He choose? You may be surprised.

The woman Jesus chose to address that day at the well was a very flawed character — at least to our way of thinking. It is amazing that she was even still alive. She had gone through five husbands, and it was both Jewish and Samaritan custom to stone a known adulteress. A barren woman, however, could easily have been married five times and survived. She would have been shamed, but allowed to live. This must have been the case with the famous woman at the well.

I knew a Jewish woman of prominence in Israel who was divorced for this very reason. Even after she was in her seventies, she still grieved at times for the husband she had set free to seek a bearing wife. Jesus dealt very compassionately with those who were affected by this cultural phenomenon (see Matthew 5:31). He was not for adultery, but He was also not against women ... and there, in His Sermon on the Mount, He was not formulating new laws concerning divorce. Rather, He was rebuking the hardened hearts of men who had no love for barren or otherwise-unproductive women.

Jesus gave only one New Testament law — that of love. The limitless depths of God's love should flow like a river through our hearts and explode like an ocean upon hurting humanity. In judging hard cases, the question should always be: What would love do? *Ha Shamayim* is an ocean of love.

God loves His first bride, Israel, and will yet draw her heart back to Himself. This is made evident in the Song of Solomon. He also loves the barren Church and yearns to impregnate her spiritual womb with a seed of the love of the Holy Spirit for lost souls. He wants intimate fellowship with her and resulting multiple new births. He reaches out to the unloved.

Jesus knew very well the situation of the woman He now called to give drink to the thirsty. The current man in her life was not one of the five husbands, but another man entirely. He may well have been a relative who knew her and took pity on her. Nevertheless, that fact was embarrassing.

For all intents and purposes, this woman was an outcast. Perhaps shunned by village women who were blessed with husbands and children, she came to the well alone that day. But Jesus "read her mail." He knew all about her. Still, He did not condemn her. This led her to realize that He was indeed *"a prophet."*

Why was Jesus asking a broken woman for help? He was looking for a yielded vessel that could be remolded and used to carry water, not only to Him, but also to a dying and thirsty world around Samaria's parched hills.

It has always been rare to find a vast supply of water in the arid land of Israel. Abundant rain has come only in times when the Hebrew people were walking in a right relationship with God. In those seasons, God sent the rain as part of His covenant with His people. When they were disobedient, He sent none, and the crops could not be harvested. Thus, the people would be judged of unholy living and sin in the Feast of *Shavuot*, or seven weeks, which comes in May or June, only seven weeks after the resurrection of our Lord Jesus on the Feast of Firstfruits. It was a judgment: to award water or not.

 He wanted a yielded vessel that could be remolded and used to carry water, not only to Him, but also to a dying thirsty world around about.

Sin always brings destruction. The *Shamayim*, the liquid glory fires of God, never bring blessing to a deceitful people. God's rain may fall on just and unjust alike, but while one may find the water sweet for harvest, another finds it bitter in floods.

In 1986, on my first visit to Israel, I heard Jewish men chanting one evening during the Feast of Tabernacles. *"Mayim! Mayim! Mayim!"* (Water! Water! Water!) They were dancing as rabbis prayed for rain, and they searched the barren drought-ridden sky for even one cloud. There was nothing. The very next day, however, as I headed out to the bus stop, a short, but drenching downpour suddenly hit. As I stood there, soaked, the scene on the street was one that I remember vividly. People began running out of their houses chanting, *"Mayim! Mayim! Mayim!"* They shouted it with jubilation, and they were revived in the downpour.

Next to my feet, a cardboard box sadly wilted in the rain, disintegrating into the gutter in minutes. The same outpouring brought both blessing and destruction. Some things ripen in the latter rain, and some things are judged, never to be seen again.

Today, Israel's desert blooms in fulfillment of ancient biblical prophecy. However, in 1990, millions of new immigrants began to worry officials in the Israeli government. As they joined the Jewish and Arab populations already multiplying within the land, would there be enough water to maintain such a burgeoning population? Environmental experts urged Israeli politicians to forge peace agreements with their neighbors in order to secure water rights. The discussion of such rights, however, complicated already difficult diplomatic relations, resulting in increased military tension. One of the negotiators, Syria's King Assad, died on the Feast of Shavuot, as he was discussing the issues relating to these water rights on the phone, saying his last words, "This is our destiny."

Near the time of the signing of the Oslo Peace Accords, God sent the *"ness"* [5] (miracle) rains in 1992. The drought was broken, and the rain came in both constructive and destructive ways. Record floods exceeded anything Israel had seen in more than a hundred years. Could it have been that God was letting the Jewish people know that He alone controls the headwaters of the heavens over that land?

Israel received such a lesson in ancient times of worshiping Baal, the water god. That they might repent and recognize the true provider of their water, the prophet Elijah shut up the heavens and forbade rains to come for three years. During the time of drought that ensued, God fed His servant Elijah beside a flowing stream ... until it too dried up. It was then that the prophet was compelled to believe for the miracle of rain. Truly, only God Himself can control the headwaters, or *Shamayim*, of Heaven over the land, the *Oceans of Glory*.

When Jesus told the Samaritan woman that He had the kind of water she was looking for, and a vast supply of it at that, she knew that He was either a lunatic with a foolish claim, or He was God Himself, incarnate as Messiah, speaking to her. Only God had such power. Only He can release the spiritual and physical blessings of *Shamayim*.

Let us believe God in the coming days to bring down Holy Ghost rains of blessing over our respective nations. They will come only in the old-fashioned way — as we stay on our knees before God, beseeching Heaven for a new song and a fresh outpouring.

Our modern sanctuaries are as fine as any that have ever existed. Our music is now very professional and sometimes rivals anything on the secular market. But if our congregations lose the desire to expand beyond their comfort zones, we are in danger of allowing the joy of our prosperity to rob us of our true potential. God's best is yet to come. We must never forget that some of history's most glory-filled meetings have been held in tents and in barns. I praise God for the prosperity that has improved our sound systems, given us excellence in music and made it possible to broadcast our wonderful sermons, but the highest technology for reaching Heaven is still on our knees!

 The highest technology for reaching Heaven is still on our knees!

Out of God's vast supply, His *Shamayim* headwaters, "liquid glory," His eternal unsearchable depths, He created Heaven. He is all-knowing, all-seeing and almighty, and He has *Oceans of Glory* ready to send rushing in upon us NOW!

ENDNOTES

1. C.G. Bevington, *Remarkable Miracles*, Bridge Publishing (South Plainfield, NJ: 1992).
2. From a message taped during the AFCM Family Reunion 2000, P.O. Box 2330, Branson, MO 65615.
3. David Baron, *Israel in the Plan of God*, Kregel Publications (Grand Rapids, MI, 1983).
4. F.F. Bosworth, *Christ, the Healer*, Fleming H. Revell Co. (Old Tappan, NJ: 1974).
5. *Ness* is Hebrew for "miracle."

FIVE

SOUNDS OF OCEAN GLORY

For with thee is the fountain of life: in thy light shall we see light.
Psalm 36:9

When I was a child, my sister Meg and I would play with Mother's collection of seashells. We would cup them to our ears and say, "What does the ocean sound like?" We could hear the faint rushing of the wind and the tide inside ... or so we thought. But that sound only made us long for the real thing.

God is *Oceans of Glory,* not a mere river. The fathoms of His depths know no sounding, nor His boundaries any end. The consuming fire of His presence, light, dances with fluid rhythmic motions upon the eternal flow of His glory through all of time and timelessness.

And God's light also has a voice. Yes, you read right. Light, an element of the manifested glory of God's being, has a voice. The rhythms of it have been scientifically measured, although not yet in totality. At the subatomic level, light waves and sound waves flow together as cosmic fluid in harmony like an eternal river of water, a light wave traveling on a sound wave known to scientists as a "quark." It is the elastic band that holds space and time together.

Those who know Genesis 1:3 already know what a quark is and what it does: *"And God said* [a sound wave], *Let there be light* [a light wave]: *and there was light."* All of the substance of creation came from that action. A light wave traveling on a sound wave produces matter, as seen in the creation story of earth and man. Jesus is *"the true Light, which lighteth every man that cometh into the world"* (John 1:9). That is physics made easy.

The quark, or the "voice of light, " is one of the most amazing elements of creation. It is the hidden trigger to creation. We can observe its behavior in a scientific field of study called quantum mechanics, which examines these obscure puzzle pieces of the subatomic realm of physics. These tiny, invisible working parts of the universe that God created would be in operation below the noise level of existing instruments that could hear them. It is strongly believed that a world of minute and infinite sounds exists there, and not only in the great expanse of space beyond us.

The Pentagon has spent large sums of money to listen in to outer space. I wonder if they know *whom* they are listening to? The same voice is speaking to us in our spirits for free.

The Jews I have met in Israel all know about "the voice." They are peculiar to other races of people on this planet in the fact that they can hear it from birth. Why? They are God's chosen people, and He speaks to them — even in captivity. They have never forgotten the voice that spoke out of the pillar of fire as it led them through the wilderness — their light in darkness.

Albert Einstein, a Jew, could hear that voice. He heard it as he meditated on Newton's theories at night, lying on a hillside flat on his back, staring up at a starry heaven. Stirrings came to his heart, he said, and he heard it when he pored through the Torah and scientific journals, laboring over the theory of relativity.

If you record a voice and play it back at greater volume, it is no less the same voice than when you play it at a mere whisper. God said, *"Let there be light,"* and the voice of light, the Holy Spirit, is still talking. Inside the atom, at the subatomic levels, *"Light be!"* and at the farthest reaches of the universe, *"Light be!"* and inside of man, *"Light be! Let there be light! Come to the light! Jesus is the Light!"* No matter where man turns, through a telescope or through a microscope, God is still speaking. The question is, are we listening?

Maybe we are, but not all on the same level, and not all are conscious of the quest they are making. But man cannot outrun the light or its voice. Everywhere he turns, the sounds of glory are calling him, "Come to the light! Come to Jesus."

Not one move in that direction will escape God's ear, for He is monitoring us better than we are monitoring Him. Had Adam never fallen, God would have delighted in showing him all the hidden world of science that man now explores alone. He knew how to create and repair it all. Everything, in the final triumph, will be reconciled to the obedience of His voice.

 But man cannot outrun the light or its voice. Everywhere he turns, the sounds of glory are calling him, "Come to the light! Come to Jesus."

God's light speaks to us consistently like the lapping tide. If we will listen to its rhythm and be led by the Holy Spirit, then we can harness the creative power of its voice. We should dominate the secret of the quark, learning to say something on a sound wave filled with Holy Ghost fire that, on a light wave, can produce things that come to pass. That is to harness the greatest power of the universe. If we can harness the tongue, we can use it like the rudder of an ocean liner in the *Oceans of Glory.* (See James 3:2-6.)

This principle of the quark is changing our modern world. The quark is found at the most fragile point in the subatomic structure of the universe, a point where matter can suddenly become a "something" or a "nothing." This is as near to the point of creation as we can imagine, because quarks are composed of "electrons" and "protons" that sometimes act like "motion waves" and, at other times, as stable unexcited dead particles. Subatomic particles do not behave in any pattern similar to the mass of the objects they compose as a whole. All objects emit frequencies of sound that sonar can detect. The spark of one minute sound can change everything. God knew that. His voice was the Big Bang!

Satan knows that. This is why he fears the faith-filled words a believer speaks. He knows just how fragile his facade is. Though death looks solid, this universe is subject to change in an instant. God's word will change it, and your words can affect it too.

Things are not what they seem. For instance, an antique wooden table appears to be the same solid treasure that it was in Grandma's day a hundred years ago. Under a high-powered microscope, however, it can be seen that the table is actually made up of a fluid substance of activity that never stops moving or changing. Though the wood no longer lives, and it is disconnected from the sap of the tree from which it was cut, atoms still exist within each cell, and their electrons and protons continue to move and rotate around a nucleus within. Rocks have the same activity at the subatomic level, and so do the steel beams of skyscrapers. Nothing about this three-dimensional world is as solid as it seems.

How very easy it is for God to remold it all or any part of it in an instant! All He has to do is bombard it with the sound of His glorious voice, and matter changes in obedience to what He calls it to become.

 Nothing about this three-dimensional world is as solid as it seems.

NASA measures the sound waves of stars and quasars. Did you know that they sing? Their musical vibrations of light can be heard with high-tech equipment. God mentioned this audible element of light to Job, a man of very primitive times:

Oceans of Glory

When the morning stars sang together, and all the sons of God shouted
for joy.   Job 38:7

A November 2, 1999, article in *USA Today,* "All the Answers for All Time in
One Tiny Package," stated that a new day is dawning when men will no longer
revel in their abilities to computerize our world with microchips, but will actually surpass that technology by harnessing the "voice" of the atom and its
electromagnetic signals. The atom itself, microscopically small, will actually
program and motorize the computers of the twenty-first century, replacing the
digital microchip. [1]

SOUNDS OF OCEAN GLORY CHANGE OUR WORLD

Imagine the changes this will bring into our world! Instead of carrying a
palm or laptop computer, we will insert coin-sized CDs into wristwatch-sized
devices.

It is fun to think that perhaps the Book of Life is as small as or smaller than
these quantum computers. I doubt that God needs St. Peter to haul around a
"clunky" scroll or some vast volume when He examines our lives to see if our
names are recorded there. It is all instant knowledge to Him. We treasure
many outdated images of Heaven in our minds because we adore tradition,
but God will change it all with a single blast from the last trump. That heavenly sound will be as significant as the first one He uttered on the day of
creation: "Light be!" [2]

Sound and light make up an "undivorceable" marriage that parents the
realm of physics (the science of matter and motion). From the center of Himself, God emanates both. Lasers of glory that stream from Him either alter or
stabilize every existing thing — according to His sovereign will.

A laser is defined as "a high-intensity beam, producing narrow uniform levels of light." In it, large, innumerable portions of concentrated light particles, or
"photons," all function on the same frequency, like a radio station. They emanate sound that can be measured by "quantum principles" and harmonize as
billions of tiny voices blending as one.

The subatomic world is a great symphony that human ears cannot yet hear,
but God hears it all — the sounds of *Oceans of Glory.* He even hears one small
drop of water as it slides off the tip of a stalactite inside an underground cave,
thousands of feet below the surface of the earth, and splashes, "kerplunk!" into
an undiscovered subterranean river. You and I cannot hear it, but God does.
Lasers of light and sound can be so powerful that they dissolve metal, yet doc-

tors use them to perform delicate eye surgery. Harnessing the power of this subatomic element of our Creator has benefited humanity immensely.

 The subatomic world is a great symphony that human ears cannot yet hear, but God hears it all — the sounds of *Oceans of Glory*.

A mirror of this principle behind the laser can be seen in a few recorded moments of history. Joshua was able to harmonize the voice of Israel. In silence, the Israelites emitted no sound for seven days as they marched around the city of Jericho. On the seventh day, in one harmonious voice, they shouted with trumpet blasts and disintegrated the stone walls of that fortified city.

I know a powerful woman of prayer who frequently fasts her words for days on end. She will not speak to anyone during those times, only to God. You cannot even get her to communicate in an emergency (except by notes), once her vow is made for the set "fast." I used to wonder about this strange custom, until I witnessed the power of answered prayer in her life.

 To speak only in the glory is a lofty goal, but it is necessary for any vessel of God who hopes to ever obtain a miracle ministry of power, signs and wonders.

We are often frustrated when our prayers and declarations of faith fail to come to pass. The greatest reason may be that we do not segregate our words, those we mean to come to pass from those we speak carelessly. Jesus was a man of few words, and He encouraged His followers not to be snared by the words of their mouths. They should let their *yea* be *yea* and their *nay, nay,* He said. To speak only in the glory is a lofty goal, but it is necessary for obtaining a miracle ministry of power, signs and wonders. Our focus is to be in the Word and have the Word in us.

Sounds That Bring Miracles to Pass

The principle of focused and unified waves of sound may be seen in some of the ministries of great healing evangelists. They understood the need to have choirs singing and congregations joining in worship for hours at a time. When the pitch of their harmony reached a high point, angels could often be heard among them. This phenomenon is recorded in the diaries of Maria Woodworth-Etter, for example.

Kathryn Kuhlman would not enter the auditorium until the proper pitch of glory was reached. When it came, she could sense the heavens were open, and then she could gracefully call down the needed miracles.

In my own times of worship and ministry, I have learned something of this secret. If I will sing a supernaturally high and focused note, it is as if lasers of light emanate from my diaphragm toward Heaven. Sometimes, with the gift of discerning of spirits, I have seen those piercing notes blast holes through the tightly woven webs of principalities and powers in the heavenlies over a city. Those anointed sounds and light affect their molecules and scramble their circuits. They are paralyzed, as beings of darkness, for a season while we are ministering there.

I feel that God is glorified in the voice, and I have learned to yield to Him in unusual realms of sound. Because of this revelation, here are just a few of the wonderful experiences that God has given with supernatural volume and pitch in singing:

- •Sometimes these high notes are so strong that they break the pointers on soundboard VU meters. In 1998, the manifestation of His glory (through my voice yielded to Him) blew out the sound system of a commercial theater in Pittsburg, Kansas.

- •In March of 2000, as we sang the Doxology, "Holy! Holy! Holy!" His glory filled my voice, and the resulting sound blew out the batteries in a man's hearing aids. His ears were healed. I was not using a microphone, and he was seated at the back of the large auditorium at White Horse Christian Center in West Lafayette, Indiana.

- •In 1998, while singing the same song in Malaysia, the unction came to set the microphone down on the stage as I continued. To everyone's shock, the volume only increased ... ten times more! The pastor and his wife fell prostrate on the floor, while a hundred and fifty people saw legions of angels for hours. When the hotel owners came to turn our volume down, they were shocked at what they heard and saw.

- •In 1999, once again in Malaysia, ministers of that city asked God to use my voice to "pierce the heavens" with praise in preparation for a first-ever healing crusade in the one-hundred-thousand-seat outdoor stadium of a Muslim city later that month. Without a microphone, my natural voice became supernaturally charged with glory and could be heard clearly on the far side of the arena. At the end of "How Great Thou Art," a fine golden sheen of light glistened on the skin of each of our hosts. It thickened, until it looked like cosmetic powder that their nightly showers did not remove for days. The heavens had burst open upon us.

•In 1995, in Oswego, New York, Dr. Flo Ellers was a witness to what happened. She writes: "Shelli asked me to join her in ministry prayer lines. I was expecting to help her lay hands on people, when all of a sudden, she started singing 'Mine Eyes Have Seen the Glory' ... . When she got to the word 'glory,' she held that note for a long time ... in a very high, shrill voice. I glanced at her and wondered, *What is she doing?* The note went on for two minutes, and then 'BAM!' the lady she was ministering to hit the floor without anyone having laid hands on her. I thought, *Now I've seen everything!* It was a glorious sound."

•In 1981 and, again, in 1987, there were two separate instances when hundreds of wild birds flocked tightly around as God led me to sing notes like these for nearly four hours in worship.

•Many times we have witnessed the glory cloud, a white mist, hanging over a congregation as the level of their worship hits that certain "pitch" of unity and purity before the Lord.

•In 1987, in Houston, Texas, I was asked to close a service, singing in tongues. We were so raptured in the glory of the atmosphere that God provided notes which the piano player testified were higher than those on the keyboard. About that time, we heard a scream. On the highest note, a man in the audience had suddenly felt a new fuzz of hair pop up on his bald head!

•On Channel 11, a PBS station in Tulsa, Oklahoma, in February of 2000, a program declared how levels of sound pitches matched various levels of light in the color spectrum. In the experiments, these waves of sound and light pierced the interior of cell walls and eliminated bacteria, virus intruders and even cancers. Is it any wonder the hair grew back?

•Dr. Paul Challgren and his wife told me of an exhibit in Chicago that showcased the sound of DNA, the language that encodes our cell tissue. A scientist had mapped the signals for a normal cell versus a cancer cell. When the signals were played through a synthesizer keyboard, the healthy cell was melodic, but the cancer cell was full of morbid discord.

•In 1994, I received a healing from a four-centimeter mass in my abdomen, not through surgery, but through massive doses of a brilliant treatment — the Word of God that is medicine to all our flesh! In listening to Dodie Osteen's testimony and healing scripture tape in the background twenty-four hours a day for nine months, my faith exploded with expectancy, not only for my own healing, but also for others'. Eighteen years earlier, Dodie had been given up to die of metastatic cancer of the liver. There was no hope! But she understood the scriptural promise that says God's Word will not return to Him void, but will accomplish the thing unto which He sends it. I believed it too, and it worked. Not only did the words build up my faith, as I listened to them over and over again, but even at night, when the volume was minimal for sleeping, the Word was bombarding my cells and encrypting my DNA with a new healthy strain for life (see Colossians 2:14)! New handwriting! New codes! God's Word is light. Light has a voice! DNA hears it! These are the sounds of *Oceans of Glory*!

Are these things new? No! In the Great Awakening of the 1700s, Benjamin Franklin was converted to Christ when he put the voice of his friend George Whitefield to the test. While George was preaching to a crowd of thousands (with no microphone, of course), Ben was measuring out the distance from the city where the mighty orator's glory-filled words could still be heard: one mile, two, three ... almost five! Mr. Franklin could still hear the convicting salvation message. Like Christ, preaching to the five thousand, Whitefield thundered with Heaven's roaring ocean sounds.

Most men today cannot preach to a crowd of a hundred without the security of a sound system. What will they do when the glory suddenly draws crowds like flocks of birds? They will need a miracle to *"be instant in season and out of season,"* to preach to all who hunger. It will happen — a sign and a wonder!

I found an interesting account in an ancient commentary on the Bible that was contemporary with the patriarchs, when the Torah was just being written. It did not become part of the Bible, but was referred to in Joshua 10:13-14 and 2 Samuel 1:17-19. In this book, *Sefer Yasher* (Hebrew for "upright account"), you can find the following observations of those who witnessed the events of the Bible in their day.

Evidently the sons of Jacob uttered no ordinary war cry. Theirs was filled

68

with glory and terrified their enemies more than the rest, with a peculiar sound that brought the physical manifestations of God's power:

> *And the inhabitants of Arbelan heard the noise of the shouting of the sons of Jacob, and their roaring like the noise of lions and LIKE THE ROARING OF THE SEA AND ITS WAVES.*
>
> *And the sons of Jacob returned against the men of Gaash who were with them from without the city, and they smote them terribly, as striking against gourds, and they could not stand against the sons of Jacob, for fright and TERROR HAD SEIZED THEM AT THE SHRIEK OF JUDAH.*
>
> *And the shriek was heard at a distance, and all the inhabitants of Succoth heard it, and all Egypt quaked at the sound of the shriek, and also the walls of Egypt and of the land of Goshen fell in from the SHAKING OF THE EARTH, and Pharaoh also fell from his throne upon the ground, and also all the pregnant women of Egypt and Goshen miscarried WHEN THEY HEARD THE NOISE OF THE SHAKING, FOR THEY WERE TERRIBLY AFRAID.* [3]

It reminds you of what happened at Jericho, doesn't it?

Whether on the subatomic level of humanly inaudible sound, or through the amplifiers of earth's loudest sound systems, all of creation will one day praise the Lord. And not one vibration will slip His attention.

When a piercing note accomplishes a breakthrough in the realm of the Spirit, I see Heaven opened, and I know it is the time to pull forth the miracle power of God for the people. But our launch window is often very short because of our short modern attention spans. People need to learn to wait upon the Lord again.

> *EYE HATH NOT SEEN, NOR EAR HEARD, NEITHER HAVE ENTERED INTO THE HEART OF MAN, the things which God hath prepared for them that love him.*
>
> 1 Corinthians 2:9

ENDNOTES

1. Pulsating laser beams of light waves would act as the switch to turn the atom on or off like a motor. The electron of a tiny hydrogen atom would become the storehouse that replaces silicon chips in current computers. In its most relaxed position, the electron's signal might be measured at a zero. But awakened by the beam of a laser light wave, the electron would become energized and emit a sound frequency on a level of a one or higher.

   Hydrogen is one of the elements of water (H_2O), the *Ha Shamayim* of Heaven's *Oceans of Glory*. **Every time you pray, you expel moisture out of your mouth. Trillions of hy-**

drogen atoms are coming out of your breath, pulsating and speaking on a level that you can't even hear, independent of your conscious words. We would fear to hear all that God hears.

The voices of millions of hydrogen atoms compacted into a space as small as the head of a pin could be used to record infinite amounts of information. Quantum computers operating on this system will far surpass the speed and memory capacities of our current computers. Not only will they revolutionize industrial technologies, but medicines as well.

2. See Genesis 1:3.

3. *The Authentic Annals of the Early Hebrews: Also Known as the Book of Jasher (Sefer Yasher)*, Morris Publishing (Kearney, NE: 1995).

CHAPTER

SIX

LIQUID GLORY FIRES

By faith we understand that the world was created by the word of God, so that what is seen was made out of things which do not appear.

Hebrews 11:3, RSV

God *"calleth those things which be not as though they were"* (Romans 4:17), because they are. There are light and sound waves and fluid substances all flowing together in the mysterious world beyond our human perception. It is foolishness to insist that these natural and supernatural realms remain categorized in separate and "unmixable" arenas, as if we could not access them both.

Albert Einstein said, "Science without religion is lame. Religion without science is blind." Some of the very people who have yearned the longest for creative miracles to visit their generation have now begun to reject them in ignorance of God's Word and of the scientific principles that lend credence to such things. A half-century ago, polio victims died when they rejected the vaccine that Dr. Jonas Salk invented. These people did not believe in the nonsense of a miniature germ world. So, what we do not see or know *can* harm our faith to receive the answers we yearn for.

Whereas some clergy were afraid to tread upon the mysterious lapse of order from the perfect world of the Creator mentioned in Genesis 1:1 to the chaos of Genesis 1:2, Einstein and others dared to pry it open for a better look. The result was that they revolutionized our world.

The twentieth century gave us nanotechnology, the new science of miniature things. Germs were discovered, and the intricate language and handwriting of microscopic DNA. The digital computer age evolved into part of our daily lives because of scientists who understood how to measure the quantum properties of different gases emitting various levels of light and sounds that could be decoded into digital signals. This work yielded the now-famous microchip, the miniature device that runs everything from heart pacemakers, to watches, laptop computers and space shuttle rockets. And, beneath this finite layer, men continue to probe even more minute, deeper levels of creation.

Scientists call the nothingness, or *"void,"* of Genesis 1:2 a "quantum vacuum" and see there the power generator for a multitude of technologies and physical and spiritual realties worth exploring. A "nothing" in the language of quantum physics does not mean the same as "nothing" in conventional terms.

Many of the conventional schools of both science and theology need to be reexamined regularly. We must take the limits off of God and never be guilty of supposing that we know it all. In the *"void"* of Genesis 1:2, there is endless cause for pausing meditation and a focused call for man to realize that we must search the depths of God. He shows His glory on the surface of life and in great depths below it where His awesome sovereignty may be seen.

 We must take the limits off of God and never be guilty of supposing that we know it all.

At the subatomic level, life is fragile at best, held in tact only by the "glue" of God's will and presence, just a spark away from annihilation. There, atomic particles wait for a spark of energy (a "quark") to either lunge into a forward motion wave of substance or decrease backward into the state of a black hole.

The place of existence where subatomic particles either become substance or lose form and mass is a negotiable space of explosive potential where anything could happen at any time. [1] That level of the universe is the most volatile of all, like an unpredictable volcano.

A black hole is a void, a chaotic place where energy and mass become so dense and unordered that even light cannot ordinarily pierce it. The ebb and flow of light, its presence or absence, affects the entire balance of the universe. Circulating like liquid glory fire from the throne of God, it blesses or judges, gives or withdraws life, according to God's Word.

Lucifer discovered this when his well-ordered kingdom disintegrated faster than the speed of light. It had all seemed solid to him, as he ruled it in great pride, but it was actually extremely fragile. How many souls have gone to an eternal Hell with Satan because their fragile lives were snatched away tragically before they made Christ their Lord! *Nothing is forever.*

Albert Einstein realized this, as he studied the *"void"* of Genesis 1:2 and summarized it in the most famous quote of the twentieth century: $E = mc^2$ **(energy [E] and mass [m] / light [c] are related)**. Without God's energy, the presence of His glory, mass is nothing — void. This helps me to understand the nature of miracles and how they form from the supernatural realm into our natural realm. Physical laws obey spiritual laws that mirror the Creator Himself. He is a

God of divine order, and all things that are natural (or appear as mass) obey Him, the supernatural source of all energy. His Word is law.

The first law of thermodynamics states that energy and matter cannot be created or destroyed. They can only be converted into one form or the other. [2] God is the essence of all of this, and all things issue forth from Him.

Energy and matter cannot be destroyed, only converted, so the Creator [3] did not invent new energized matter but created or drew [4] that which existed out of Himself into this realm. He, God Almighty, is the absolute constant of the universe.

 Energy and matter cannot be created or destroyed, only converted into one form or the other.

Many theologians believe or, at the very least, seriously consider the idea that God never created anything chaotic. So how did the perfect earth and heaven of Genesis 1:1 become null and void? It is believed that when God destroyed the throne of Lucifer, it became a black hole, or a "nothing," or a "void." It did not lose the codes of its DNA; it only lost its order and energy levels to exist in a coherent form. This was a catastrophic biblical event that God was able to fix.

And the earth was without form, and void; and darkness was upon the face of the deep. And the Spirit of God moved upon the face of the waters.

Genesis 1:2

In that black hole, or fallen world, would have also been the DNA of everything that once existed there — matter and energy not destroyed but converted into a nonsubstantial format, until the Holy Spirit moved over it and the glory-filled voice of God awoke it all, calling it back into being.

"God calls those things that be not as though they were." If He called an ocean to be, then it answered Him and appeared at the speed of light out of that black hole. If He called a tree, bird or dinosaur, its DNA, its matter, its energy, its essence answered Him. What an awesome moment the angels enjoyed, watching as God created our current world, arranging these elements in divine order!

"Light be!" Beginning at the speed of light, each "thing" proceeded from the mouth of God, winding down into slower earthly atomic revolutions, until it reached the set boundary levels of what earth was called to be. Thus, they materialized into a perceivable solid form. Particles of energy and matter obeyed the language of their coded substance, DNA. Out of the "nothing," they returned, and of those things that be not, something appeared.

DNA is the handwriting that encodes every cell. It tells an eye to be blue, or a body to be tall and to mature. It is a great mystery to us, but not to the Potter, who can smash a universe and begin again from the same clay. Apparently, He did it all once before and can do it all again, as He will in the re-creation of the world.

By faith we understand that the world was created by the word of God, so that what IS SEEN WAS MADE OUT OF THINGS WHICH DO NOT APPEAR.   Hebrews 11:3, RSV

And, Thou, Lord, in the beginning hast laid the foundation of the earth; and the heavens are the works of thine hands: They shall perish; but thou remainest; and they all shall wax old as doth a garment; AND AS A VESTURE SHALT THOU FOLD THEM UP, AND THEY SHALL BE CHANGED: but thou art the same, and thy years shall not fail.   Hebrews 1:10-12

The volatile force of light existent in the universe was meant to remain constant in motion and in order, in a perfect cosmic space. That would describe the liquid glory fire of God. Its disruption would be similar to watching a live high-voltage electric wire become disconnected as it falls to the ground and sparks begin to fly in a dangerous, wild and unpredictable arc.

Lucifer's rebellion ripped and confused that order, and his fall caused a cosmic decrease in the levels of light and the velocity of it. This could be attributed to the existence of such things as black holes. [5] When Satan fell down on the job of maintaining the harmony of the throne of God, he really "messed things up" (see Ezekiel 28:14-15).

Regardless of how the perfect world of Genesis 1:1 became the *"void"* of Genesis 1:2, it was not what it had been intended to be. Rev. Billye Brim, who is my favorite eschatology teacher, relays a German student's understanding of the Hebrew phrase *"without form and void"* (*tohu va 'bohu*). "You have cleaned your house until it was perfectly spotless, and then you open the door of your teenager's room, and you scream, 'This place is *tohu va 'bohu*! Clean it at once.' These rhyming Hebrew words mean — *tohu:* formlessness, confusion, unreality, emptiness, chaos, waste, and *bohu:* emptiness. [6] Isaiah 45:18 shows that God didn't create earth in vain (*tohu*), but formed it already perfect, ready to be instantly inhabited. God's work is perfect (see Deuteronomy 32:4). God's work is glorious (see Psalm 111:3)." [7]

So the "nothing" that God created our earth from was anything but a quiet placid space to begin with. Within it was a seething, confused mass of elements that could neither be created nor destroyed, but only rearranged. Fallen angels must remain chained there, while other elements were called out of it to become part of a refurbished planet, which God designed Adam to guard from the fallen ruler, Lucifer, Satan, or the devil.

Whether the book of Genesis is actually the story of Creation or Re-creation, it really does not matter; the creative miracle principle is the same. As God once created it, He could just as easily have re-created it, as He will again on the day of resurrection. Out of the dust of the earth, the depths of oceans and all places where human remains are scattered, God will rearrange the matter and energy and call the elements to be whole again, in the twinkling of an eye, in a sub-atomic second.

When God formed man of the dust, He may have literally been digging for something precious in there. Perhaps there was already a DNA chain dormant, scattered within the dust from the perfect order of the world that God had originally made in Genesis 1:1 and that He wished to recall, creating a man who would *"replenish"* the earth. If so, God will just as easily recall the missing parts in this day for re-creative miracles, and one day He will do the same for the whole human race, either with glorified bodies or the second death.

THE CONSUMING FIRE OF HELL

I don't ever want to go back to the black hole of Hell that I once visited as a teenager one night in a near life-and-death experience. (Please see the testimony of that experience in the final part of this book.) I want to be thrust forward into the glories of eternity with Christ. But there is coming a day when all that is not to be re-created will, once again, be sealed into a black hole, a nothing, a void, a chaos. This time, God will not speak to it; He will not visit it or have fellowship with it. In the final judgment, the energy and matter consigned to the void will remain forever locked away from God's presence and light. It will never be converted to life again. And the glory of the Lord will fill all the earth, and time will be no more.

When God fills up time with His glory, and time is no more, then He will consume it and everything left within it. Adam was created to be a timeless immortal. When he sinned, his days were suddenly numbered, and man began to count time: time until redemption, time until death, time until resurrection, time until *"the end of time."*

Birth pangs of TIME seized the earth, and the contractions have become shorter and sharper with catastrophic events. One day, the last birth pang will strike, and the very end of TIME will be birthed unto us. Then, *"time shall be no more."* No one in Heaven or earth will be able to find TIME. It will be known, but not found. Those souls who are caught in the darkness of the black hole of Hell will continue to count *TIME* as though they could ever escape its confines, knowing that they never shall. No intercessor will weep for them, for, in God's mercy, tears for them will finally be wiped away from the eyes of all who live in heavenly joy, and the lost shall eternally be forgotten by their Creator and their loved ones.

And the consuming fire of Hell ... ? What shall it be? Satan has no fire, no light, only utter darkness. In eternity, he will own nothing at all. Inside the heat of the Light of Lights, the Glory Himself, the lost will all be withdrawn into nothingness and there eternally burn, consumed by their own Creator. They will know themselves in that place called Hell and be forever tormented by TIME that cannot be ended. Their tormentor, Satan, will be locked away with them all the TIME. Their cry will be, "Oh, I thought I had more TIME, and it ran out. It sealed up! I am trapped! Let me out! Let me out! Let me out!" But God alone will hold the key that shall never let them out. Every atom and molecule in the universe shall obey Him and get into perfect order, and they will cover up the damned and consume them, as though they had never existed. Hell will be consumed in the Lake of Fire, and our God is a consuming fire of liquid glory (see Hebrews 12:25-29).

Hell will be a horrible place where all matter and energy will disintegrate to a very different level of existence than that of the persons allowed to have glorified bodies and live in the presence of God face-to-face in eternal joy. Were it not for God's mercy, none could survive His glory. Were it not for His love, we all could have remained a void of particles floating in that black hole of Genesis 1:2. But from the foundations of the earth that He created (or re-created from it), we were known and called forth in the dust of Adam's DNA, of his loins. Aren't you glad?

LOVE IS A CONSUMING FIRE

God is love, and His heart yearned for us to come forth. Over that negotiable space of Genesis 1:2, the Spirit of God hovered and brooded with knowledge of all the elements contained therein, including man. He contemplated how He would reorder it all, and when that was complete, He spoke on a sound wave that penetrated the black hole, followed with a light wave — "Let there be light!" — and substance was formed. An orderly planet came into being in six days out of the chaos, as the eternal goodness of the vast *Oceans of Glory* poured forth through that voice.

And God said it was *"good."* ("Good" is *tov* in Hebrew, the totality of all that God is, all His love.) The breath from this same voice of the Holy Spirit breathed into man, who then became a living, speaking soul. [8] And this love God desired to share with man, created from dust.

A rabbi once told me that the Hebrew word for this marvelous dust was best defined as "the smallest traceable particle of matter." How fine is a piece of dust? Under a microscope, it is able to be divided as small as an atom, which some scientists now declare has no point of condensing. The atom is bottomless, and so is God. He has no beginning, nor end.

CYCLES OF LIQUID GLORY

by Shelli Jones Baker © 2000

1. The heavens were saturated with the glory,
the liquid glory, the shed blood of the Lamb,
from the foundations of the earth.
It poured into earth's one vessel meant to
contain it — A-dam!

2. Adam falls. Abel's blood cries out from
the ground. Its voice is heard by God.

3. Life is in
the blood.
It flows through
biblical
history in bulls,
goats, doves and lambs.

4. The Light of the World
enters the womb
of a virgin.

5. The sinless blood of Jesus is sacrificed.

6. Jesus,
our High Priest,
pours
His blood
on the
Mercy Seat of Heaven.
Man is redeemed!

7. The latter rain of glory
begins falling
toward earth again,
to fill up 120 fasting,
praying
vessels with the power
of
Pentecost.
As the cycle
of the blood
and
the glory
fills them, they begin
to pray with
glory-filled
voices!
Heaven and Hell are
shaken
with the language
of the blood
(see Hebrews
12:23-29)!
Rivers
of revival
come forth
— and
Oceans of Glory!

77

If you were to label the smallest particle of dust A and the farthest reach of the Universe Z, you and I exist somewhere in between — and so does God. Not only is He big, but He is also small and also just your size, in between those two extremes. He is the same size as every cancer cell. He is not far away, out in space, but near to you, closer than a breath away.

One word from God can change anything. This same voice of the Holy Spirit was breathed into man, who became a living, speaking soul. We are created to speak such words of faith and to dominate chaotic circumstances. To no other creature was this ability given. In the twinkling of an eye, faith-filled words can change subatomic realities and manifest solid miracles. Hallelujah!

Similarly, what all two thousand years of Church history put together could not manage to accomplish, God, in the last great revival of all time, will accomplish in seconds. Human lives and eternal destinies may be altered beyond all of our calculations. Jesus WILL have a holy, united Bride. He may send a flood of ocean-sized glory waves, an outpouring of liquid glory fire that will purge the stoniest heart in seconds, a bonfire of Holy Ghost combustion! God is the Master of the quick conversion of nothing into something.

 What all of two thousand years of Church history put together could not manage to accomplish, God, in the last great revival of all time, will accomplish in seconds.

Einstein understood, in part, how much energy could be converted into atomic particles to accelerate past the speed of light and disappear. Most men have never been able to test that theory yet, but Enoch, Elijah and Jesus did. They were all raptured in their bodies and taken to Heaven in a burst of glory, where fiery chariots, or angels, were seen.

Isn't it interesting that the generation that curiously devours every bestselling novel on the Rapture also yearns to understand the greater scientific realities of the theory of relativity that Einstein left us?

"In a moment, in the twinkling of an eye," a subatomic second, [9] we will be called by a supernatural sound wave, the trump of God, and will fly to His presence faster than the speed of light, [10] vanishing in the Rapture and reappearing in the clouds of glory!

"Enoch walked with God and was not." The two of them walked together at the speed of light and glory. Enoch was permanently translated to Heaven, as his body was flooded with the consuming glory of God. Liquid fire consumed his blood, and he yet lives. Man was created to walk with God, in the depths of His glory; therefore, we should view every devastated human life as a black hole, with possibilities waiting to be called or recalled to life in Christ! We should emulate the Father, Son and Holy Spirit, as, with compassion, they seek to res-

cue drowning sinners sinking into Hell. The anointing on our lives can reorder their circumstances, to provide a way of escape.

LIQUID GLORY, OCEANS OF RAPTURE

Jesus' faith reordered the surface of Galilee's turbulent, stormy waters to accommodate both His weight and Peter's. But when Peter broke that connection with the glory all around Jesus, he found out just how fragile the heavenly flow was. He immediately began to sink.

When Peter put his eyes back on Jesus and took His hand, he was flooded with the glory and experienced another instant change. The *Shamayim* of Heaven is a volatile, continuously-moving force of subatomic realities that may or may not be seen and may or may not materialize, but God wills it to be seen for a person who reaches up with the voice of faith.

Faith is placed in an agitatable state of being when it is characterized by the changing variable known as "NOW." This is an arena where the past can change and the future be altered. *"NOW FAITH IS ... SUBSTANCE!"*

 Faith is placed in an agitatable state of being when it is characterized by the changing variable known as "NOW."

Now faith is the substance of things hoped for, the evidence of things not seen.   Hebrews 11:1

Interestingly enough, Einstein stated that light was substance. When God's glory touched chaos, it gave it substance, form and weight. Recently, Scottish physicist Peter Higgs added insight as to how this happens. His discovery, known as the "Higgs boson" or the "God particle," is a subatomic particle responsible for giving all matter weight and the spark to become a "something." *Kavod*, the Hebrew word for glory, meaning "weighty," "heavy," describes this. Glory has weight. (That sounds like the *Ha Shamayim* of Heaven, *Oceans of Glory*.)

 When God's glory touched chaos, it gave it substance, form and weight.

The "God particle" (the Higgs boson) is soaked up by other subatomic particles as by a dry sponge, causing them to become as water-laden, weighty. It is believed that the Higgs particle floated in a primordial soup, a fluid mass of unattached matter and energy in a black hole where everything needed for the order to sustain the life of the future was preexistent within the chaos. Scientists are taking a deeper look into the fluid, ever-moving, minute base of all creation with atom smashers. God is providing the technology, or the camera, to take the snapshot, and many are yearning to use it. *"Deep calleth unto deep."* God is saying, "Come find Me."

> *No man can come to me, except the Father which hath sent me draw him: and I will raise him up at the last day.* John 6:44

The Omega Point Theory, written at Tulane University by Frank Tippler, claims that the Higgs boson was the loving genius spark of God that caused the Big Bang of light to burst forth from the chaos in an orderly, lawful fashion. I believe that the "God particle" is "the speech" or "glory-filled voice" of God. The eternal pronouncement of His voice is an unfading signal that continually energizes all matter into a stable condition. The judgement of His voice might sound like a supernatural sonic boom, which could easily vaporize it all. [11]

It is obvious to the scientific world that now embraces the Higgs factor that a God of divine order governed the creation of earth and Heaven and everything inside, below, and beyond it. Hallelujah! How exactly God chose His words! We should imitate Him. We are the clay vessels, the fountains through which God will fill the earth with a release of liquid glory fires, rivers of revival, *Oceans of Glory*. When we speak His Word, our voices fill with glory and dispel the darkness with light.

Einstein said that light was a material that possessed mass and weight. He theorized that there was an existence of a fourth dimension, where time is absent and eternity reigns. It existed, he said, in the realm of light and was higher than the three-dimensional realm of light velocity in which this universe exists. Therefore, it could only be pierced by an object traveling at the speed of light.

The sound barrier, likewise, can only be penetrated by an object traveling at the speed of sound. When this occurs, there is a sonic boom. We could thus theorize that when an object pierces the light barrier, there should be a burst of light. This is exactly what the biblical writers recorded as having happened with the appearance of angels. Many testify of a bright light or fire bursting around them or those who minister to them. Jesus is the Baptizer with fire! This phenomenon has been recorded often throughout Church history.

Someone will record the Rapture too. We will travel at the speed of light and beyond, when the liquid glory fire of God consumes us and flows in our veins at the Rapture. This will be like rocket fuel in us, as we shoot through the heavens and pierce the veil! The last trump will be the loudest sound ever. If there are witnesses to that burst of light in the heavens, they will know that we left in a flash and also will know where we went — UP!

The absence of the weight of glory invites the weight of sin, the density of death. When Adam became weighted with sin, he ceased to be immortal and became mortal, remaining earthbound. When the glory has filled the Church in her final hour, it will cause every weight to be set aside, and she will become Heaven-bound, every molecule rearranged for the ascent. No one will get air-sick or fall behind in the middle of the Rapture. God can arrange the smallest atom and the largest galaxy and carry us in the palm of His hand. He comprehends and measures the weight of all things — the weight of glory or the weight of sin.

 ### Jesus is the Baptizer with fire!

God loves the scientist, the common man and the theologian alike. He is interested in drawing them together and to Himself. He wants them to hunger for a snapshot of that moment of creation. One day in eternity, it will be His supreme joy to show us all how He created the world that He explained to Moses, who recorded the visions of his audience with God on Mount Sinai, while the mountain was consumed with fire. He was caught up in the *Shamayim* of Heaven, flowing backward on that eternal river to see eternity past and to record creation. This liquid glory fire that flooded the veins of Moses then shone from his face from the inside out, until it had to be veiled (Exodus 34:29-35).

Jesus, too, tapped into those *Oceans of Glory* on the Mount of Transfiguration. The Shekinah glory of light not only illuminated His flesh, but soaked also his clothing. Jesus must have been glowing again the day He walked on the water, for the disciples thought that He was a spirit — a ghost, phantom or angel — and not a human.

Jesus was flooded with glory. After His resurrection, He was often of a form that caused His best friends not to recognize Him. The living water and light of Heaven illuminated His being and changed His countenance. He needs His followers to be flexible too, craving the fullness of Heaven's eternal flow, the liquid glory fire that moves us into the limitless depths of God.

We must get to the place that we can say, "All things are possible" and mean it, because we see it and know it. Holy living and a hot pursuit of God will keep this spiritual connection open. Sin will dam it up, restricting the blessings from an open Heaven to a mere trickle.

What a mighty God we serve! The *Oceans of Glory* that He is sending upon us will bring vast and sudden change. He does not enjoy dead things, for He is life. He is moving, and there is a constant flow of power in His creation. Nothing about God stands still or sleeps or dies, and it never will.

Our God is a consuming fire, an eternally flowing fountain of glory. Let the liquid glory fires of God move you and consume you.

ENDNOTES

1. Of the *"void,"* cosmologist Andreas Albrecht says: "In the quantum vacuum, there is actually a lot going on ... . It's a very interesting place where it is never impossible for a universe to start." USA Today Tech Reviews by John Yaukey, Gannett News Service, 11-23-1999.
2. Lambert Dolphin, a physicist who also happens to be a Christian, suggests that "even in the absence of matter, empty space possesses potential energy." This obeys the First Law of thermodynamics. Dolphin also suggests that the fall of Lucifer, the archangel of light, forced the universe to get rid of excess energy, thereby causing light levels to change. Lambert T. Dolphin, *Jesus, Lord of Time and Space*, New Leaf Press (Green Forest, AR: 1988).
3. OT:7069 Creator: *qânâh* (kaw-naw'); a primitive root; to erect, i.e., create; by extension, to procure, especially by purchase. (Biblesoft's New Exhaustive Strong's Numbers and Concordance With Expanded Greek-Hebrew Dictionary, copyright © 1994, Biblesoft and International Bible Translators, Inc.)
4. To draw out; by extension, multiplication, extraction or expansion from one original source.
5. Confirmed by the research of Norman and Setterfield on the theory of tired light. Abstract by Norman and Setterfield, *Tired Light:* "The behavior of the atomic constants and the velocity of light, C, indicate that atomic phenomena, though constant when measured in atomic time, are subject to variation in dynamical time. Electromagnetic and gravitational processes govern atomic and dynamical time respectively. If conservation laws hold, many atomic constants are linked with C light. **Any change in C light affects the atom.**
    For example, electron orbital speeds are proportional to C light, meaning that atomic time intervals are proportional to $1/C$. Consequently, the time dependent constants are affected. A systematic, nonlinear decay TREND is revealed by 163 measurements of C light in dynamical time by 16 methods over 300 years. Confirmatory trends also appear in 475 measurements of 11 other atomic quantities by 25 methods in dynamical time. Analysis of the most accurate atomic data reveals that the trend has a consistent magnitude in all quantities.
    Lunar orbital decay data indicate continuing C light decay with slowing atomic clocks. A decay in C light also manifests as a red-shift of light from distant galaxies. These variations have thus been recorded at three different levels of measurements: the microscopic world of the atom, the intermediate level of C measurements, and finally on an astronomical scale. Observationally, this implies that the two clocks measuring cosmic time are running at different rates.
6. Francis Brown, *A Hebrew and English Lexicon of the Old Testament, Based on the Lexicon of William Gesenius*, Oxford University Press (Oxford, England).
7. Billye Brim, The Blood and the Glory, Harrison House (Tulsa, Oklahoma: 1995)
8. Divine inspiration and intellect made him a speaking soul. As a baby learns by imitating a parent, so Adam spoke as God spoke to and through him. His speech was filled with glory and creative power! OT: 5397 Breath: *neshâmâh* (nesh-aw-maw'): from OT: 5395; a puff; i.e., wind, angry or vital breath, divine inspiration, intellect, or (concretely) an animal: KJV - blast, (that) breath (-eth), **inspiration, soul, spirit.** (Biblesoft's New Exhaustive Strong's Numbers and Concordance With Expanded Greek-Hebrew Dictionary, copyright © 1994, Biblesoft and International Bible Translators, Inc.)
9. *Moment* in Greek is *atomo*, where time can no further be divided.
10. 186,300 miles per second, the speed of light.
11. USA Today Tech Reviews, *Seeking the Missing Subatomic Link*, by John Yaukey, Gannett News Service, 1-19-2000.

LOVE LIKE AN OCEAN

HERE IS LOVE [1]

1895, the Welsh Revival

Here is love, vast as the ocean, lovingkindness as a flood.
When the Prince of Life, my ransom,
shed for us His precious blood.
Who His love will not remember,
who will cease to sing His praise?
He will never be forgotten
throughout heav'n's eternal days.

On the mount of crucifixion, fountains open deep and wide.
Through the floodgates of God's mercy
flowed a vast and gracious tide.
Grace and love, like mighty rivers,
poured incessant from above.
Heaven's peace, and perfect justice,
kissed a guilty world in love. [2]

God's *Oceans of Glory* are the limitless depths of His love. Where the river only provided waters enough for us to swim in, the ocean will baptize us over our heads in a revival of love for lost humanity. With breakthroughs of vast and inexhaustible resources to traverse the leagues of distance between God and man, we will enjoy the ocean even more than we have the river. "More, Lord!"

The very thing that has kept God at a distance from the humanity He created is love. His love, His glory is a consuming fire; it consumes sin. Were God to consume earth with His presence before the time appointed for the end of all things, it would mean the annihilation of most of the human race. But where sin abounds, God's grace abounds *"much more"* (Romans 5:20). That grace is a protective cushion of mercy over this planet right now. It allows mankind to seek God in an imperfect state of being. This cushion has come to exist in the Church age — the very age of grace — because of the blood of Jesus:

> *But if we walk in the light, as he is in the light, we have fellowship one with another, and THE BLOOD OF JESUS CHRIST his Son cleanseth us from all sin.* 1 John 1:7

One day man will again be privileged to intimately know God in the fullness of His love, the limitless depths of the *Oceans of Glory*. This experience will go beyond the rivers of revival outpourings and Holy Spirit baptisms. In that day, we will live in glorified bodies, free from our sin, judged once and for all, forever sealed into the presence of God. God will walk and talk with us, as He did with Adam before the fall.

Why was sin able to break the bond of love they shared? Sin is a state of being in which the human soul and spirit are out of the flow of divine order. Sin stems from rebellion and cries out to be corrected. Sin is like a magnet to the righteousness and divine order of God. It begs to be judged.

Sin is also like a sinkhole in the bottom of the sea. As it opens up a void when the earth's crust shifts and quakes, it invites the ocean above it to fill and consume it. The love of God, the *Oceans of Glory*, will find sin and consume it, like water rushing into any empty hole — if we allow it to happen. People cannot repent of sin unless convicted with the love of God.

 Sin is like a magnet to the righteousness and divine order of God. It begs to be judged.

Sin carries you further than you wish to go and keeps you there longer than you want to stay. In 1975, I heard Evangelist Billy Graham give "the two-second test" to a group of college students. "It only takes two seconds," he shared with them, to ask yourself: "Would Jesus say this? Would Jesus drink this? Would Jesus smoke this? Would Jesus enter this doorway with me? If Jesus came for my soul right now, would He approve of this activity I am engaging in?"

It is for this reason that I love the WWJD bracelets and T-shirts that have become so popular in recent times. The question "What would Jesus do?" has become "the two-second test" for the teenagers of today. Many will see Heaven instead of Hell because of that simple phrase. [3]

Only by mercy does this world of thieves, adulterers, sodomites, liars and idolaters exist. God yet longs for the souls of man to repent and turn to Him:

> *Be patient therefore, brethren, unto the coming of the Lord. Behold, the husbandman waiteth for the precious fruit of the earth, and hath long patience for it, until he receive the early and latter rain. Be ye also patient; stablish your hearts: for the coming of the Lord draweth nigh.* James 5:7-8

Because God is eternal, He can more than afford to be patient. That is why He did not immediately swoop down on Adam to rescue him from his sin. He questioned Adam, and out of his own mouth, the man confessed his sin and snared himself in it. As a result, the barrier was fixed between man and God. In order to mend the broken relationship (albeit in stages), God slew animals to cover the fallen human race with blood. He removed Adam from eternity and Eden, posting an angel at the gate with a flaming sword. That angel yet guards the gate to that realm from which man is forbidden. It exists, though unseen.

How can this be? God did not vaporize Eden. It still takes up three-dimensional space on this planet, yet in our high-tech world, we cannot find it. Praise God, there are still mysteries that the Almighty conceals. We only discover what He allows. I see how this hidden realm exists when I think of the example of my laptop computer.

Through it, I can access a wealth of information. By using the modem and connecting to the Internet, I can literally access the accumulated knowledge of the world (as much as is on-line, of course). However, unless I split the screen or use various windows, I cannot view more than one file at a time. Hundreds of data files exist on CDs, Internet servers, hard drives, zip drives, ditto or jazz cartridges, which can be accessed, but only if I know how to find them.

When the power to my computer is turned off, the screen goes blank and reveals no clue to what lies within the reach of that seven-pound box. There are entire realms of words and images that exist, but they are hidden from my senses. In this same way, Eden, Heaven and Hell exist — all at once — hidden from the naked eye, perhaps occupying the same space all at once. (This world is definitely not what it seems to be.)

For instance, Jesus may have ascended through the very gate of Heaven itself, an opening in Eden hidden from human view, a place the angels guard with flaming sword, barring all unworthy visitors. From that location of the Temple Mount, Calvary, the Kidron Valley and the Mount of Olives, Jesus prayed, was crucified, ascended and will return. (This geographical area is not more than two miles wide as the crow flies.) On this same mountain area, King David purchased the threshing floor of Onan the Jebusite, after the angel of the Lord appeared there. It was in that location that fire fell from Heaven to consume the sacrifice that Solomon made when the Temple was dedicated.

And why that location? Jewish sages say that Adam would have recalled the location of his birth, for he arose from the spot a full-grown man. [4] God then marked it as holy, the portal between Heaven and earth, the precise location where He breathed Himself into humanity. Surely, Adam would have returned as close to that location as possible with his sons to sacrifice. It is a special place. It may be the navel of the black hole turned inside out, where God said, *"Let there be light!"*

But wherever Eden, or Paradise, is located, God keeps it hidden and secret, so that man cannot further corrupt His universe. Yet Adam was created to explore it all; it was his inheritance.

How the heart of God longed to draw Adam back to Himself! But, alas, He could not. Had He reached down to kiss that "boo-boo" of sin on His fallen son, His love would have consumed the man, for Adam was now full of the very thing God's glory consumes — sin! Instead, wisdom demanded a carefully orchestrated legal plan to bring man back to the point of grace from which he had departed. Because of this, the Messiah was prophesied to Eve. God had a remedy that would be revealed in time.

After Adam fell, God was in somewhat the same position as are the mothers of children born without immune systems. These mothers can never touch their children, for their expressions of love would be the kiss of death, ending the very lives of the ones they long to caress.

I read about these lonely "bubble babies" in *Life Magazine*. A small percentage of infants born into the world have no immune system, and they lack the ability to develop one. No vaccine or medication seems to help. From infancy, such children are forced to live in a plastic bubble, much like a gigantic incubator. The air they breathe is purified, and they must have special food and water. Their diapers are changed by gloved hands inserted for this purpose through the walls of the bubble, and any contact with other humans must be through this plastic barrier. This becomes the total existence of these children.

It is because of this that children born with such a limitation normally do not live past the age of puberty. It is not, however, a failure of the bubble that finally claims their lives. It is their determination to escape the confines of the bubble that usually kills them.

For instance, one twelve-year-old boy felt trapped inside that bubble and deprived of the most important elements of life. He could observe his parents and siblings, speak to them and watch TV with them, but always from within the confines of the bubble. He could eat his meals at the same time they ate, but he had to remain inside the bubble, and they had to remain outside of it. He could never actually touch his parents or siblings.

Eventually, the boy shattered the bubble himself and broke free from it.

Hours later, after he had kissed every member of his family, he died because of disease contracted from germs in their breath. The isolation of the bubble was more than he could bear.

God, our heavenly Father, longs to consume us with His love, but He cannot do so until the sin in our lives is finally put under the feet of Jesus. Eventually, He will give us glorified bodies so that we can once again withstand the totality of His glory. In the meantime, a measure of His glory is available to us in this life, by the presence of the Holy Spirit, who quickened Jesus from the dead and now quickens our mortal bodies. He has shed His love abroad in our hearts and given us but one law to live by in the New Testament — the law of love.

A Jewish friend of mine who lived in Israel once told us that she felt sorry for Christians. When we asked her why, she replied; "I have more than six hundred laws to live by. God knows that it is impossible that I should ever keep them all perfectly, and so He gives me the Day of Atonement once a year. Jesus gave you only one law, and it is the most difficult of all." She was referring, of course, to Jesus' command that we love God and that we love our neighbors as ourselves.

Her observation was profound, for the ocean of God's love that has been given to us through Jesus represents the totality of that which was the aim of all the Law and the prophets. We were not intended to think of how we could break the existing laws or circumvent them. We were to live them all. This impossible task could only be done by the working of the Holy Spirit, putting God's love within us and engraving His law upon our hearts:

> *And hope maketh not ashamed; because the love of God is shed abroad in our hearts by the Holy Ghost which is given unto us.* Romans 5:5

The King James Bible mentions the word *love* three hundred and ten times in the New Testament alone. The apostle John even devoted an entire epistle to the subject. He has come to be known as "the apostle of love," for he walked in so much purity of that virtue that boiling oil could not kill him.

To a man of that depth of love, God poured out more than a stream of revelation; He opened up an ocean. The book of Revelation scopes the timeline of the ages of human existence into eternity and has captured the heart and imagination of every generation. Countless volumes of commentaries and recorded debates have been published on that one book of the Bible, and they may even outweigh the libraries of books written about the Old Testament, the gospels and the epistles.

 To a man of that depth of love, God poured out more than a stream of revelation; He opened up an ocean.

Love, the Law of the Angels, [5] written by my good friend Dr. Gwen R. Shaw (a veteran missionary of more than fifty years), is on my list of recommended books for all who would be soul-winners, revivalists or pastors. How can we believe for revival in our land if we do not love souls?

The key to the Welsh Revival was a focus, not only on prayer, but on the subject of divine love. Wonderful hymns were written on that theme during the revival.

Christians have not always been loving, either to saints or to sinners. During the Reformation, many were martryed for their faith. Martin Luther, who knew what it meant to be persecuted, forgot the feeling when he wrote of hatred for the Jews and also for Catholics in his latter years. The people of England, Germany, Rome and France led the way in religious wars for centuries. Bloody battles ensued over such topics as the canonization of the Scriptures and their publication and distribution, as well as about the proper way to pray.

Many Christians have a mixed record in Heaven when it comes to love. The infamous slave traders of the 1500s, Sir Francis Drake and Sir John Hawkins, were considered by many of their peers to be fine, upstanding Christian men. At the same time they were enslaving men of another race, they were also conducting religious services onboard their ships, hallowing Bibles in the captain's cabin and using their ill-gotten money to fight the Pope and support the Puritan Protestant movement. When they were at sea, they had a young evangelist preach every day at high noon on the top deck and forced the captive audience of officers, shipmen and slaves to listen — at gunpoint. How ironic! [6]

Many unwise and overzealous acts have also been performed in the name of love, but love is never haughty, rude, selfish or boastful. When these things are present in us, we have departed from God's love. This is a serious matter, for although Jesus was *"approved of God ... by miracles and wonders and signs"* (Acts 2:22), John taught us clearly that we will be known in this world by our *"love"* (John 13:35).

The limitless love of God caused Corrie Ten Boom to embrace one of the hated Nazi guards (who were responsible for her sister's death) as a new brother in Christ and to forgive him. She understood that he did not know what he was doing. In the hysteria of war, he had carried out Hitler's instructions mindlessly.

The love of God caused a woman whose husband had been killed by a drunk driver to give the culprit a home after his prison term had ended. Her love and witness made such an impact on him that he became a preacher. The oceans of God's love will drown every offense — if we allow that love to be fully *"shed abroad in our hearts."*

Love has caused many missionaries to surrender their lives so that some lost tribe could gain Christ. This makes me to realize that many of us yet lack love.

Until a burden for lost humanity consumes our every waking hour, as it did with Jesus, we will never have enough of His love. His entire life on earth was lived for that one cause. His great love counted us all as valuable and precious — unconditionally. God loves men and women, even when they have rejected Him and died and gone to Hell. Let us be filled with love for all those for whom Christ died.

 Until a burden for lost humanity consumes our every waking hour, as it did with Jesus, we will never have enough of His love.

Many powerful biblical passages exhort us to love. Several come to mind: Matthew 5:43-44, 22:37-40, John 15:10-12 and 1 Corinthians 13:1-8. Get ready. Those *Oceans of Glory* filled with God's unconditional love are coming our way. Nothing can separate us from the love of God.

ENDNOTES

1. Words by William Reef and William Edwards. Music by Robert Lowry.
2. This song is in the public domain. If you would like to order the music, please e-mail us.
3. This slogan has been revived from one first made popular in the 1920s.
4. *Newsweek* magazine, July 24, 2000, "The Real Jerusalem," by Daniel Klaidman and Jeffrey Bartholet.
5. Gwen R. Shaw, *Love, the Law of the Angels,* Engeltal Press (Jasper, AR: 1974).
6. John Sugden, *Sir Francis Drake,* Henry Holt & Company, Inc. (New York, NY: 1990), p.7, p.95, p.100, p.171.

EIGHT

A CREATIVE MIRACLE WAVE

Ye men of Israel, hear these words; Jesus of Nazareth, a man approved of God among you by miracles and wonders and signs, which God did by him in the midst of you, as ye yourselves also know.   Acts 2:22

Although love is always the most important fruit we expect from the manifestation of God's glory, He is also showing us many different signs and wonders and miracles, some of them new and quite unexpected. These are a display of His power and glory, the overflow. Until a tsunami hits a city, most men have no idea what it even looks like.

You can't swim in a puddle; you have to go where the deep water is. Set your faith to get into the ocean, and God will get you there. You have to go where the glory is manifesting and see the miracles. God wants you to be blessed.

It would take an entire book to recount all of the many miracles and signs God is revealing to us today, but allow me to tell you of just a few.

I have already mentioned the hair that popped up on a bald head at the singing of one high note, and I believe we will see more of this phenomenon in the coming waves of the *Oceans of Glory*. We will also see withered arms shoot out, crippled legs able to walk again, spinal cords healed and other great miracles.

 You can't swim in a puddle; you have to go where the deep water is. Set your faith to get into the ocean, and God will get you there. You have to go where the glory is manifesting.

In 1999, at Ashland, Virginia, during a campmeeting, Ronnie and I preached on creative miracles side-by-side in twin pulpits as a tag team. (Sister Ruth Heflin had prophesied that we should.) The people had come from around the globe for an eleven-week span of miracle services, and we were finishing it up on the tail end, upon a foundation built all summer by wonderful healing evangelists and teachers. Expectancy was very high in that atmosphere before we ever spoke a word. That fact was a key ingredient in their being able to flow in the stream of creative miracles.

The camp dinner bell rang on time for dismissal, but the people began, in one unified voice, to cry out, "We did not come to eat. We came for miracles!" Someone in the crowd began singing in tongues spontaneously, and everyone joined in. Over the next three hours, some glorious miracles sprang forth.

Twelve people testified on the platform that day of restored knee joints (they ran around the large tabernacle). A broken foot was made whole in its cast. Three deaf ears heard. A Scandinavian man with mammary cancer (such as is usually suffered by women) lay slain in the Spirit for five hours, while new flesh could be felt growing back upon surgical wounds and two egg-sized tumors disappeared from his collarbone. We had hit a vein of glory as the oceans poured upon us! [1]

 Expectancy was very high in that atmosphere before we ever spoke a word. That fact was a key ingredient in then being able to flow in the stream of creative miracles.

Knee Joints Re-created

The healing of the knee joints is another of the very unusual miracles we are receiving on a regular basis. We prayed for a women not long ago who had her knee joint surgically frozen after an accident. She had been in great pain for years and desperately wanted to be healed. God did the work that day. Many others were healed that night and received creative miracles in their knees.

It was so easy to get people healed, for the atmosphere was pregnant with miracles. I called for all the hardest cases, and people with every type of severe need came forward and received.

The next day, Sister Gwen Shaw asked me, "Why knee joints? Last year God was healing thousands of teeth and filling them with gold ... and still is, but why the sudden rush of re-creative miracles in so many knee joints?" (We have had twenty-six such healings since August of 1999.) I believe these are the reasons:

- First, God wants to heal knee joints because He loves those who are in pain.
- Second, it is to show men and women that their knees are ready for bending at altars of prayer.
- Third, God will send those with renewed knees to run among the nations and carry the Gospel during the great harvest of the whole earth.

I was doubly thrilled by what happened with one of those miracles of renewed knees. It was Saturday, February 5, 2000, and Judith Moore of Columbia, Missouri, came to one of our meetings for healing. She once had cancer, and a portion of her knee joint had been removed. I was tired after a week of preaching and, sensing no great anointing remaining upon my weariness, was also doubtful that we would have the desired miracle. I began to caution the woman about what she might need to do in further preparation, in case she did not receive. Then the Holy Spirit stopped me and told me not to say those things anymore. It was cowardly on my part and destructive to her faith. It was a new day, and the Spirit was going to work for this woman.

I prayed for her, saying, "Knee be! Substance be! Now faith is the substance!" As I prayed, a tangible anointing, consisting of a light-filled dust of a golden hue, appeared on my hands, a creative miracle substance that had begun appearing out of nowhere. I had once read about a green light appearing in the hands of William Branham, and of another healing evangelist whose hand would glow red hot when the Spirit of the Lord was present to heal. This thrilled me with encouragement to continue commanding her new knee to manifest.

Something was happening, and it raised my faith level. If God could do anything as amazing (to our minds, at least) as that, and out of nowhere, then He could re-create the woman's knee. I suddenly realized how the bone cells and other tissue needed to restore that body could manifest through the atmosphere and move from the throne room of Heaven to earth in a matter of mere seconds.

It took a little patience on my part, but within ten minutes or so, the miracle came. Suddenly, the woman's missing kneecap buckled up under my hand and popped into place, and she "took off," jumping and screaming, and running by her friend. The friend told me, "She can't do that! But she's doing it."

The next thing we knew, this woman with her brand-new knee had run up on the platform and thrown herself down hard on both knees. She threw her hands up in the air and shouted, "Thank You, Jesus, for my brand-new knee! I've been wanting to pray to You on my knees for five long years! Thank You, Jesus!" In August of 2000, I saw Judith again, and she confirmed that she was still enjoying her new knee. Hallelujah!

That act was even more touching to me than the miracle of her healing. Her desire at that moment had been to fall on her knees and express her gratitude to God. Her shouts were explosive to those who had lingered for prayer after the meeting. To me, that woman was like the one leper out of ten, whom Jesus had healed and who came back to praise Him. The Bible says that *he* was made whole. He was the only one who went further. The others received only new skin, but he must have received a new nose, new fingertips and new toes — or whatever else he needed!

 Her desire at that moment had been to fall on her knees and express her gratitude to God.

Golden Glory Dust

The manifestation of the "gold dust" is one of those totally unexpected miracles that leaves everyone who sees it speechless. I don't even like to cheapen the miracle by calling the substance "gold dust," because it is so holy and more like a three-dimensional, golden-colored light.

We first saw the most vivid modern-day outpourings of this when we were with our friend Ruth Ward Heflin in Israel at one of the oldest churches in Jerusalem, where she was ministering one night. It appeared on the faces and hands of everyone who was there, including the surprised pastor, who became instantly "drunk" with joy in the midst of that traditional service.

Why would God do something like that? What would be the purpose? The Lord immediately answered me, reminding me of a visit to Heaven He had allowed me in 1983. [2] It had occurred as a result of falling into a trance while singing the name "Jesus, Jesus, Jesus" for four hours at a service with Pastor Terry Mize and Mama Carmen Goodwin of Tulsa, where we were praying for missionaries worldwide. When I arrived in Heaven, everything I saw around me was gold, even the water, which seemed to be alive and musical and had an amber glow to it.

Jesus said to me, "When I took you to Heaven in 1983, what did you see there?"

I answered, "Gold! Everything was gold."

He replied, "Some believers are now pressing so close to Heaven, as the veil stretches ever more thin, that a residue of gold from My presence, the glory, is remaining on them. That is what is on your hands! Rejoice!" I did.

The "gold dust" began to appear on us more consistently that fall, and it has not ceased since that time.

Dusted With Miracles

As for the earth, from it comes bread,
But underneath it is turned up as by fire;
Its stones are the source of sapphires,
And it contains gold dust. ...
What is hidden he brings forth to light.

Job 28:5-6 and 11, NKJ

The "gold dust," or "glory dust," comes in two forms that I have seen — through the pores of the hands or other parts of the body, and as a fine rain from above. In the hands, it begins with a few tiny sparkles, and as you literally stand there watching, it multiplies before your eyes. Once, it seemed to be as thick as a plastic glove and was oily in appearance. On some people, it can be more coarse, but on most, it is very fine.

Some might suggest that this is normal, for the body has a tiny bit of gold in it (chemically, naturally). It is a known fact that gold is one of the body's own healing agent minerals, and doctors use gold shots for relief of arthritis. What we are experiencing, however, is much more than normal perspiration could produce.

This gold is also not the same dead yellow as golden jewelry or glitter spray. It has a very distinct look to it. If you look at it closely, you can see that it is definitely three dimensional. Each tiny flake is shaped like a diamond, but because it has an amber glow, it is more like a million tiny lights. This light part of the manifestation is what amazes me most.

Many people are calling this phenomenon "gold dust," for lack of a better term, but it is actually something much more unusual. Gold dust doesn't come and go, but this substance does.

I find this substance on my hands, most often while I am in my private times of fellowship with the Lord. Sometimes it lasts for hours, and sometimes only minutes.

 It is a known fact that gold is one of the body's own healing agent minerals, and doctors use gold shots for relief of arthritis.

In the second manifestation of the "gold dust" that I commonly see, it begins to rain down from nowhere. It comes in a thick, pouring stream, proceeding not from the ceiling, but from several feet over the head of the person who is ministering, over others on the platform and even over those who are seated in the congregation. It covers, to various degrees, their hair and clothing.

Some people collect this "gold dust" in their Bibles or in some prayer cloth. After we had caught it the first time in Ronnie's Bible, we allowed dozens of people to wipe some of it off in their hands, but it kept coming back, and we still had roughly the same amount as we originally had gathered.

A very dramatic incident with the "gold dust" happened with Pastor Jeff Johns at White Horse Christian Center in West Lafayette, Indiana. Ronnie had some of the "gold dust" fall on his Bible, and one Sunday morning was led to put it on Jeff's injured leg, which was stiff from a football injury. He had trouble moving it freely and standing on it for any length of time. That Sunday morning, he was healed. In the evening service, he leaped up a flight of stairs to demonstrate what God had done and testified that he had even gone out jogging earlier that afternoon after he was prayed for.

Ronnie put a little of the "glory dust" collected in his Bible on one of my paintings, *Seated With Christ in Heavenly Places*. [3] The painting was inspired by two visions — my own in 1978 of the return of Christ, and by Bob Shattles' vision of Christ upon His white steed at the gate of Heaven. He said that as the horse pawed the gold pavement of Heaven, restless to be on his journey back to receive the Church, this caused a fine gold dust to fall to earth. It was an inspiring and thrilling vision that encouraged all of us concerning the hastening hand of God. His return is surely imminent.

As I painted on the huge six-by-four-foot canvas, Ronnie was inspired to put a touch of the "dust" on golden streets beneath the horse's hooves. The "dust" adhered to the clear acrylic sealer, and then it multiplied. Someone noticed that the dust had created a reflection of the horse I had painted.

I personally know at least thirty people who experience the appearance of "gold dust" on them on a regular basis, and hundreds of others have come running up to us in church services, weeping, to show us that it has appeared on them, too.

There are also many related miracles. I saw a fine emerald dust on the face of one minister I know. Then one night a fine dust that looked more like diamonds appeared on many, and they also had an oil with a sweet, perfumey smell. I had it in my own hands in January 1999, in the healing line at Christian Life Center in Kuala Lumpur, Malaysia. I was not aware of it until some people in that very modern city church came and grabbed my hands to examine them. They wanted to know why oil was all over their faces where I had touched them.

At the time, we didn't say anything about it. I still had mixed feelings about these signs (because of the problems a similar phenomenon had caused back in the 1980s). I had read, however, that in the revival of the late 1940s, several of the very well-known evangelists had experienced this often.

A Creative Miracle Wave

The Focus Is Jesus

The gold or the oil or the diamond dust is not the focus. The focus is Jesus and the miracles He is performing because of His covenant promises in the Word. We must not commercialize this miracle in the advertisements for our meetings or use it as a badge of superiority in the ministry. It is a holy and precious thing, and we should treat the subject with reverence.

Did Jesus do miracles like this one when He was on earth? It is very possible, because John ended his record of Jesus' life and ministry by saying that Jesus had done many more miracles than could possibly be recorded:

> *And there are also many other things which Jesus did, the which, if they should be written every one, I suppose that even the world itself could not contain the books that should be written. Amen.*   John 21:25

Are people being helped by these unusual signs? Absolutely! First, they are thrilled that God would touch them in a way that can be seen and shared with others. These signs have brought a new excitement to the churches, and attendance has soared where this is happening. What God is doing is so obviously supernatural, in a world with so many skeptics and with technology that can explain away anything and everything, that it shows people that God is alive and that He loves us. This brings many souls to Christ, even among those who have been stubborn and have run from God for years.

In Maryland, a lady saw the gold on my hands, and for the first time in her life, she believed in miracles. I had been trying to win her to the fullness of Christ for years. When this happened, it quickly got her attention. She was very excited. "For the first time in my life," she said, "I have seen a miracle of God. Wow!"

The next day she called me from the hospital where she worked to say that the same "gold dust" had appeared on her hands as she was telling the nurses there about it. "What do I do with this?" she asked excitedly. The nurses were huddled around her listening to our conversation, and they began to receive the "gold dust" too, as we spoke.

I was rushing out the door to meet Sister Ruth Heflin, and had no more time to talk with them. My ride was leaving for the four-hour trip. I quickly said, "You have been touched with the same glory of God that the angels touch in Heaven. Now, go lay hands on the sick, and I'll explain more of it to you later." I have to admit that it was a very simplistic answer, but it satisfied them, and they went about their tasks with great delight.

The first woman who received the "gold dust" is now a changed person. The fact that the "gold dust" came on her before she had a chance to set her personal affairs in order obviously shows that the "gold dust" does not validate the person upon whom it appears or falls, but that the God of glory freely gives it to show His love and mercy. Why else would He touch otherwise-unrepentant sinners? This manifestation is a free sample of His love and grace. He desires to pour the whole ocean out on them — if only they can get into position to receive it.

NOTHING NEW

An old-timer, Rev. Dr. Charles Robertson, cofounder of the Great Passion Play in Eureka Springs, Arkansas, told me of the "golden rain" before he passed away. In his youth, he worked for healing evangelist Aimee Semple McPherson, performing the special effects in her famous illustrated sermons. One night she asked for rain, and he had no time to "rig up" anything. But, lo and behold, suddenly a golden rain of glory and what seemed to be droplets of real water sprinkled the people from Heaven without Dr. Robertson's help. [4] Mama Mary Jenkins, who is now ninety-two, was also an eyewitness to this. Golden rain in services is nothing new, only a sign that God has dropped one of His calling cards once again to alert us to yet another cycle of revival glory on its way.

He desires to pour the whole ocean out on them — if only they can only get into position to receive it.

AN EXPLOSION OF WEALTH

In Jerusalem, we attended an Arab engagement party, where I saw something I had not seen anywhere else in the world. When the bride came in, looking like a Miss Universe, her hair was covered with silver dust from the beauty parlor. Her individual pieces of jewelry had large nuggets of silver on them. I was stunned by the beauty of this display. The Arab women, many of whom I had seen the day before wearing their distinctive head covering, were now bareheaded, away from their men. This revealed the huge chunks of gold hanging from their ears, dripping from their necks and dangling from their arms. I would estimate the worth of each collection at $50,000 or more! It was the real thing.

The mother of the groom greeted me and explained about the gold. "This is the gold we received at our engagement parties. It is enough to sustain us in case we must one day flee our homes. It is enough to secure our futures." I had never seen gold in such large chunks. "We only wear it," she told me, "when another of our ladies becomes engaged."

The groom and the bride were seated in two chairs decorated as thrones. They exchanged her silver for his gifts of gold between them. He also sprinkled her with real gold dust from a jeweler's shop. It was awesome. Very soon now, we will be going to the wedding palace of the Lamb, and Jesus, our heavenly Bridegroom, seems to have begun sprinkling us with "gold dust" in preparation. What could be more beautiful? Hallelujah!

In 1998, the Lord showed me that if I would disregard my own dislike for long airplane journeys to Asia and go there for His work, He would double the anointing on my finances and ministry. Indeed, we watched in awe as this happened: double the meeting schedule, double the previous crowds, double the offerings, book sales and miracle testimonies. If we would receive one of any item donated to the ministry, we would receive another immediately, usually on the same day. These gifts included vans, computers and other items. Then, the following year, we began to see the double of the double, or the quadruple blessing (see Isaiah 61:7). As we prayed for others who began to have faith in this new anointing on our lives, they often received the same results.

We have enjoyed the testimonies of an African American and a Cherokee Indian, both preachers, sharing on their television programs about the supernatural wealth that the *Oceans of Glory* have recently poured out on them. They are from two of the most impoverished races on the continent, and yet by the Word of God, they have both built up a faith level to receive status among the wealthiest citizens of the nation. These are mere forerunners of what is to come!

One of these individuals gives away more than a million dollars each year to missions, and the other now drives a donated and designated Rolls Royce over the cotton fields that his slave granddaddy once worked. [5] Both men are winning thousands of souls to Christ each year. That sounds to me like the Old Testament Bible story of Joseph. He, too, was enslaved, but was suddenly freed and prospered to bless others.

 He, too, was enslaved, but was suddenly freed and prospered to bless others.

God wants to reveal Himself through us, as He did through Abraham. But He wants us to be comfortable and graceful with the wealth He brings, like Jesus, who had free access to all resources. We are not to be "nouveau riche" with it. [6] People of "old money," land and aristocracy use wisdom in how they manage it, and thus they maintain their prosperity. The richest man I ever heard of in my life was an old Arab sheik who sat cross-legged in the desert in his robes near a goatskin tent. His cell phone in hand, he kept one eye on his trusty camel nearby, and the other on CNN, received from his satellite dish. Meanwhile, his wives, in a Mercedes-Benz, sat on a dune in the distance, upon the sands of his $500-billion-dollar oil fortune. God wants to prosper us for the sake of His Kingdom better than this. Abraham and Solomon were the wealthiest men in history. We have an even better promise (see Galatians 3:13-14).

SIGNPOSTS FOR SOULS

The most notable outpouring of this "gold dust" miracle manifestation is in the ministry of our friend Rev. Bob Shattles, a retired police officer and Baptist pastor/evangelist, of Revival Fires Ministries in Georgia. He was carried away to Heaven in a service where he was hosting Sister Ruth Heflin. He tells how Jesus appeared to him and offered him more anointing to reach more souls. He accepted. When he came away from that encounter, he, too, was covered in the "glory dust." He said that the Lord told him this sign and wonder would remain on his ministry to attract curious lost souls, if he would not be embarrassed or draw back because of the criticism of skeptics.

What Bob has is very real. I have never known him to personally draw attention to it, although it does powerfully attract the lost.

I am not surprised that people who go to Heaven can come back with a little of the gold from there. After all, the astronauts brought back moon rocks, souvenirs for show and tell. Ha! Ha! In Jesus' day, those who saw His miracles ran to tell others, and so it should be today.

Many thousands of people have come to see and hear Bob preach, and many of those have come to Christ. He has also won thousands of people outside of the pulpit, one-on-one, in the highways and byways of life, as he goes about his everyday responsibilities, anywhere and everywhere he goes. I have never met a soul-winner like Bob. His love for all mankind, even those who are in a most deplorable condition, truly astounds me. His endurance to labor among them in long prayer lines through the midnight hours is also humbling.

When people come to Bob Shattles' services, they do not hear a complicated message. The message he brings is always on Jesus, Hell or Heaven, which happen to have been the main messages of the Welsh Revival and the Great Awakenings of the past. The manifestation of the glory has been a signpost for souls.

Some skeptics have missed the whole point, wanting to test the golden "dust." I wonder what they would have discovered about Moses' old wooden rod or the coin in the mouth of the fish Peter caught. Was that coin real or counterfeit? Caesar accepted it, but skeptics always want to know for sure.

I saw a report in Virginia, from a forensic lab, that showed the "gold dust" to be pure gold. But a newspaper in Dallas snubbed the sample they received as being petroleum-based, as if it were a plastic glitter. This tickled me. Don't they know that it is much harder to pull petroleum from wells deep in the ground than it is to enter the vein of a gold mine? And which of the two is more valuable?

The point is not what chemical substance the dust is made from. The point is that thousands of people are genuinely turning to Jesus because of it. The dead are being raised (and these miracles are documented), tumors are being healed and the lame are walking again. I say, "Glory to God!"

 The point is that thousands of people are genuinely turning to Jesus because of it.

A Storm Warning

My only caution would be to those who search for man-made products to imitate this phenomenon, with the intention of deceiving people. They are on very dangerous ground, like the magicians in Moses' day who mimicked the miracle of his rod turning into a snake, by doing so themselves through the work of familiar spirits. Ananias and Sapphira died from trying to lie to the Holy Ghost and His prophets. However, none of these imitations in any way discounted the bonafide miracles of God in their midst, and they certainly did not cause the people who witnessed them to become confused as to which miracle was from the devil and which was from God. The fruit spoke for itself.

A second time they summoned the man who had been blind. "Give glory to God," they said. "We know this man is a sinner." He replied, "Whether he is a sinner or not, I don't know. One thing I do know. I was blind but now I see!" Then they asked him, "What did he do to you? How did he open your eyes?" He answered, "I have told you already and you did not listen. Why do you want to hear it again? Do you want to become his disciples, too?"
John 9:24-27, NIV

One final word on this aspect of miracles: It is entirely possible to be covered in "gold dust" or oil or glory goosebumps from head to toe and not receive an ounce of healing or prosperity. It is like trying to ride a wave without a surfboard. You can do it, but only for a split second. When the touch of God comes, we must receive it by faith, build on it with faith and God's Word, and guard it with prayer and holy living. Jesus is not coming to see who is covered with "gold dust," but rather who has faith and what is he doing with it?

> *I tell you that he will avenge them speedily. Nevertheless when the Son of man cometh, shall he find faith on the earth?*   Luke 18:8

FLOATING IN THE OCEANS OF GLORY

I want to share a portion of a testimony from Kenneth Copeland's mini-book, *Living in the End-Times*, published in 1998. [7] It is from the chapter entitled "Staying Anchored in a Flood of Glory":

> I know of a church in Africa that had a great outpouring of the Holy Spirit, and the daughter of a witch doctor was born again and baptized in the Spirit. Her daddy didn't like that one bit, so he went to that church during a service and planned to curse them (and I don't mean just say ugly things to them).
>
> When he got there, there had been manifestations of God's glory in that service, and he said, "I don't care what kind of miracle you do. I'll match it!" Well, he actually pulled off a couple of things, but the devil's been doing that since Pharaoh's days. Then all of a sudden, everyone in that church building started rising off the floor and got about four feet in the air, where they were suspended ... that is, everyone except that witch doctor, who just kept running across the front of the room, jumping as high as he could. But God's presence was so strong that no one paid any attention to that old boy.
>
> Finally, all this got to him, and he fell on his face and gave his heart to the Lord. Sure enough, everybody just floated right back down.

Let's lighten up! What would we do today if, instead of laughing and being gold-dusted in churches, we all floated in midair? Most of our minds can't even begin to fathom that. If God is eventually going to rapture us, then who says He cannot float a few of us before that time if He needs to? Let's take the limits off of God!

As a child, I loved wild rollercoaster rides, but my sister did not. At Ocean City, Maryland, Mother put us both on the "Wildcat." We each experienced the same ride on the same course and for the same length of time, but I did it with supreme joy, and Meg did it with her knuckles clenched white! We still laugh over that. If God brings miracles, why not enjoy them? Hang on for the ride. It is glorious!

I have seen a vision in my prayer life, of an hour coming, in the near future, when people exiting church or tent meetings at night will do so, glowing like fluorescent bulbs. When I told this to Sharon Wells, a pastor's wife in Abilene, Texas, she responded, "Well, Jesus Himself was transfigured!" I had not thought of that in regard to what was in my spirit.

RAISING THE DEAD

There will also be more people raised from the dead before the Rapture, not only fresh corpses on hospital gurneys, but also embalmed corpses in graves — as on the day of Jesus' resurrection. A missionary told of an eighty-year-old woman in Uganda who had died at the age of fifty-six. Buried four days, she suddenly arose to testify of her visit to Heaven and lived to minister, still bearing the scars of worms that had eaten her flesh in the grave. It has happened before (see Matthew 27:52-53)!

My husband, Ronnie Baker, relays this wonderful incident that happened in Jones, Oklahoma, in 1995: A couple "living together in sin" came to hear him preach one night with their sixteen-year-old daughter. (A decade prior, in prayer, the Holy Spirit had told Ronnie to expect at least three people to be raised from the dead in his church services, mapping out his course.)

Ronnie remembers:

> In the middle of my sermon, I heard a scream. The mother jumped out into the aisle, pulling on her hair. "My daughter! She's dead!" Shelli ran back to the rear of the church and put her arms around the girl, who lay slumped over dead on the floor from an asthmatic vapor lock in the throat.
>
> Shelli yelled, "I plead a wall of the blood against you, Death!"
>
> Then I heard the Lord calmly say, "Just tell her to come back, and I'll see to it that she does."
>
> After a few minutes, I walked back and knelt down beside the girl and called out her name. I said, "You've got to come back. You can't leave this way. Come now."
>
> And do you know what? Raising all three of those people from the dead was the easiest thing I ever did. It's easier than getting some people healed. Why? The gift of faith is in operation, and there is no doubt. Their will is not involved. God removed all of my fear because I knew before I even started that it's nothing in me or about me at all; it's about Him. Jesus said, "I only do the things I've seen and heard my Father do" (see John 5:19). We did that as the girl came back from the dead.

Shelli felt the girl's chest jump dramatically as she began to breathe again. Somebody told her mother, but at first she couldn't believe it. Then the girl's eyes popped open with excitement and fear. She said, "While I was gone, I was going down a black tunnel ... . And fumes and the smell ... . And before I got to the bottom, I heard you say, 'Come back!' I don't want to go there anymore. Help me, please!"

Her mother began to cry. They all got saved in a hurry and made Jesus the Lord of their lives. That couple changed. They got married and quit living in sin.

Rev. Bob Shattles has had seven documented cases of raising the dead in the past year alone in his ministry. Eight people — doctors, nurses, orderlies and undertakers — received Christ around the bed of one of those who was raised up.

We are hearing of other such cases. What a glorious day is dawning! Rev. John Osteen of Lakewood Church in Houston, Texas, produced a well-documented video, "Death and Beyond," that verifies similar testimonies.

UNCUT GEMS

Uncut and unpolished gems have been falling in some of our meetings. Janet McArthur, of Lafayette, Indiana, showed us an amethyst in the toe of her shoe, which she had placed back on her foot after being barefoot in prayer at the altar. Pastors from Maine called to report that following our services there in April 2000, an uncut emerald fell at the altar in the prayer lines. They wanted to know why.

We can only wonder why. Just as the Hebrew children questioned the bread of Heaven that fell every morning, asking, "What is it?" (the word *manna* literally means "what is it?"), great signs and wonders are coming that none of us have seen before. We must humbly conclude that we do not know it all.

GOLD TEETH

Dental miracles of all types have become commonplace recently in many Spirit-filled circles. A church in Tulsa e-mailed me with a report of forty-five teeth filled and verified. A church in Pennsylvania e-mailed of more than a hundred and fifty sets filled. In the United Kingdom, more than three thousand believers received the same miracle in March of 2000, during a single service, publishing the report on the Internet. [8]

Those receiving these miracles are obviously thrilled and drawn to God. A dentist told me that gold is the most biocompatible substance with which teeth can be filled — other than the real thing — and some are even miraculously receiving that when their earthly budgets couldn't even afford a dentist. Cavities have disappeared, replaced by new material that looks exactly like the original tooth. Who wouldn't be impressed with a miracle like this? And what could better demonstrate God's love for us?

In Malaysia, the wife of the pastor in a church where we spoke received a supernatural cleaning of the blackened fillings in her teeth, and they turned shiny silver again. Her dentist verified the miracle the next day. In Ashland, Virginia, a woman came forward and showed me eight solid-gold teeth that she had received in a service there that summer. The dentist who verified the gold as real said that it was worth nearly $8,000 and that the work surpassed his own skills and the grade of gold in his supplies.

THE BLIND SEE, AND THE LAME WALK

At first, creative miracles just happened now and then in our ministry, but now, as I preach on creative miracles, they are happening consistently. God healed a woman's blind eye and dried-up optic nerve on February 18, 2000, in Tulsa, Oklahoma, at our People of Prayer Rally. Her name was Irma.

In January of 2000, an unsaved Mormon lady walked out of her wheelchair as I sang supernaturally high, sustained notes over her in the name of Jesus. It took twenty minutes, and the entire healing line was made to wait. But, WOW! Was it worth it! After she was healed, she wanted to get saved. We saw her again in August, and she was still healed, and here is how it happened.

HOW ONE CREATIVE MIRACLE WAS MINISTERED

In Las Vegas, there are some wonderful churches reaching out to the biggest fishpond of sinners! Like Ephesus, Las Vegas is a good place for God to perform miracles to the saving of souls.

Rev. Bertie McCoy, pastor of Echoes of Faith Church, asked me to minister there. As I started the service, it was strongly anointed in the area of healing. I began to sing "Jesus Is Alive and Well," accompanied by a sound track. I had used it many times in other services and never had such results as we did that night.

After I sang that song once, the glory rolled in, and the pastor requested it again. At that point, I knew that I would not be preaching, but felt that I should lay hands on the sick. The Holy Spirit, however, gave me a very unusual directive. As I called the sick to rise and begin to come forward in preparation for the laying on of hands, I heard Him say, "Send them back to their seats. I only want the hard cases, what an aspirin or an antibiotic cannot cure. Tell them that."

"Ohhhhhhh! No, Lord! I can't!" I protested. "What will the pastor think?" She was my friend, and I surely did not wish to damage that relationship.

About that time, Sister Bertie said, "Lay your hands on me first." She said that she was scheduled for a painful dye test of clogged arteries the next day. What I did not know was that she never allowed herself to be slain in the Spirit when a visiting minister was there. Sandy Robbins, one of their evangelists, informed me later that the elder minister wisely always "watched and prayed" from the platform. On that night, she rested in a deep trance of God's presence through the entire remainder of the evening.

As I laid my hands on her, an intense fire began to burn in them. So intense was the burst of heat that it melted the band on my wedding ring, popping it open, causing it to fall on the floor.

The pastor was completely cured that night and received a perfect health report the next day, much to the amazement of her doctors. She recently wrote that two years later the healing remains firm.

But, with her being slain on the floor, I was left alone with only myself and God totally in charge. It was a scary position, because now I could not blame my intended disobedience on the pastor. I again argued in my heart with the Lord: "Father, I have had ailments that an aspirin and an antibiotic could cure, and they hurt! I can't send those people back to their seats!"

The answer stunned me: "Whose meeting is it anyway? Yours or Mine?"

Well, when He put it like that, what was I doing there if God wasn't to have His own way? I followed His instruction, gritting my teeth. The people looked sad and disheartened, but they sat back down.

Again I called the sick to rise, but this time I stipulated that it must be for something that an aspirin or an antibiotic could not cure. This time, God added more clarification to the call: "Tell them not to come up for giving up their cigarettes tonight either. Not a one of them in this place is serious enough to do it yet. It is dangerous to play games with Me."

"Ohhhhhh! Lord," I thought.

An incident that was reported about R.W. Schambach came to my mind. He once called all the smokers to the front and said, "Repeat after me:

" 'Oh, God, if I ever ... ' They repeated it.

" 'Smoke another cigarette as long as I live ... ' They repeated it.

" 'Kill me!' " Some repeated it, but others fled back to their seats or out of the building. Wow! A wind of holiness was blowing. A river of purity was flowing.

I followed the instructions of the Lord, and now only a handful of people came to the front. God was pleased, as I heard the Holy Spirit say, "I only want the hard cases tonight. Do not lay your hands on anyone until I show you whom. The anointing in your hands is the full measure of that person's healing, and when that person receives it and is healed, all the others in the place will get the healing *they* came for."

 The anointing in your hands is the full measure of that person's healing, and when that person receives it and is healed, all the others in the place will get the healing *they* came for.

I told the people this word, and it caused the crowd to work with me in a very involved way. I later found out from eyewitnesses of the great healing revivals of the twentieth century that if they could get just one or two healed in a service like that, the rest were "a cinch." Long healing lines would then move quickly past the platforms with constant and amazing results.

Again, we replayed the sound track to "Jesus Is Alive and Well." (When the Holy Spirit lets you know that He is pleased to anoint a song, then stick with it until He lifts from it. We make a great mistake in our song services sometimes by not being sensitive to Him.) As I sang, the glory increased and blessed the people. A woman in the back of the church later said, "I have never experienced anything like that in my life. You sang in the healing line. Why?"

My answer came swiftly by the unction of the Holy Spirit: "Haven't you ever heard that God inhabits the praises of His people?" (see Psalm 22:3).

As I sang and walked up and down that prayer line, my eyes searched for the hardest case. At last I found her, a lady in a wheelchair. When I laid hands on her, the fire began to drain out of them into her back.

I heard the Lord urge me, "Do not take your hands off of her until all of the fire drains away. Therein is the full measure of her healing meted out. When she is healed, she will be like a prayer cloth, saturated with glory, and as she passes by the people who were told to stay in their seats, everyone in the building will get the healing they came for." This must have been what happened in the book of Acts, when Peter's shadow passed by people in the streets, and they were healed. He was saturated with the glory from prayer meetings.

Sick people were brought out into the streets on beds and mats so that at least Peter's shadow would fall across some of them as he went by!
Acts 5:15, TLB

It worked! She walked effortlessly, when God was through with her. Grace came in the glory. As she walked with me down the center aisle, it was as if she was one large healing cloth, saturated with the glory. People all over the church leaped up shouting about their healings as we passed each pew. Even a drunkard from the racetrack next door had been led in and was instantly sobered, as God healed his back, and he ran to the altar in repentance, of his own accord.

The grandchild of the woman tugged on my dress and cried, "Ma'am, you don't understand. My grammy is a Mormon; she doesn't know Jesus."

I said, "Well, honey, she does now!" What a wonderful way to meet the Savior — on a healing wave of glory!

This event tried our patience for almost twenty minutes to obey and believe, but all the effort was well worth it. The woman was still healed when we saw her a year later.

I think sometimes that we are so foolish to say, "Well, if God wants to heal me, He can do it anytime." Oh, really? How often have we given Him twenty minutes in a prayer line for one little elderly lady to receive like that? Most churches only give God three minutes to sing in tongues and prophesy. They must believe in the slogan "A little dab will do ya!" The problem is, it doesn't "do ya" very far. God, most generally, will not work in our ten-thirty to noon box that we try to squeeze Him into. It is very rude of us to expect that He will. Healing is the children's bread, but we have to pull up to the table! Then it is a good idea to wait until we are served.

 Healing is the children's bread, but we have to pull up to the table!

A creative miracle wave is here, but if we want to experience it, we will have to jump on the curl and ride it!

ENDNOTES

1. A full video of this service is available by sending $25.00 to P.O. Box 177, Branson, MO 65615. Ask for the title: "Creative Miracles."
2. In 1983, I was praying for missionaries at a service that Mama Carmen Goodwin took me to in Tulsa. We hit the main vein in that service and pleased the Holy Spirit, who came rushing in upon our prayers with the glory. Several of us were carried up in that service into trances, heavenly visitations and visions. I was one of them. The Lord took me up into a heavenly place as I was singing the name of Jesus. "Jesus, Jesus, Jesus ..." The name, being sung on a high pitch, activated happenings in Heaven and on earth, much as one would operate a garage door opener on a certain signal pitch.

   It was not because Jesus is some kind of egomaniac about hearing His own name. No! But it is a pronouncement of the covenant, and He wanted to teach me about the power within it. As I sang the name of Jesus, it caused the strings of heavenly harps to sympathetically vibrate and play without the touch of a human hand. (Years later, in the 1990s, a French harp company began experimenting with harps that have hydraulic systems, electronic midi boards and harmonic curves strung with only laser beams of light, no wires or gut strings. I always love it when God confirms the things He shows me sometimes. It causes me to have greater patience to believe that, in the process of time, I shall see it all come to pass, either on this side or on the other.)

As I sang the name of Jesus, the strings of the harps began to play, sympathetically activated by the pitch of my voice alone. Jesus explained, **"Everything that belongs to the sound of the last trump will come unto it. It is the most pure, the most focused pitch in the entire universe. When it passes through the earth's atmosphere, like a magnet, all that is tuned to that pitch, all that was purified by My blood, all who believed in My name will arise to its calling."** (Light has magnetic force.) He is the light of the world, and His voice is filled with the glory of that light.

Suddenly the earth below became visible to me, and I saw all those who were tuned to that pitch, living holy lives in Him, come instantly to meet Him in the air as whole human beings, resurrected, and others preceded who had been alive on earth, the resurrection of the dead, the Rapture of the Church!

3. You can order this from our website: **http://members.aol.com/shellibake/index.html.**
4. From a taped interview done during our Jones, Oklahoma, revival in 1997.
5. The IRS confirms that a designated item cannot be sold or converted to cash for any other purpose. God gave the car to the grandson of a slave to give testimony in modern times to His mighty delivering power.
6. French for "new riches." True people of aristocracy use this term in a demeaning way to describe people of new money who do not know how to use it properly, often abusing it in careless ways to be gaudy or to show off.
7. Kenneth Copeland, *Living in the End-Times, A Time of Supernatural Increase*, Harrison House (Tulsa, OK: 1998).
8. Gold teeth: We received an e-mail verifying a massive miracle of filled teeth at the "Catch the Fire" Conference in the UK with John and Carol Arnott. Attendance was said to be twelve to fifteen hundred (forwarded from petermallett@fdn.co.uk to vcf-pastors@grmi.org, dated April 14, 1999).

SLAIN IN THE SPIRIT OF THE LORD FOR DAYS

WORDS ANd MUSIC by
Shelli Jones Baker copyright 1994

Slain in the Spirit of the Lord for days, Losing all

Our car-nal ways. Slain in the Spirit of the Lord for days,

We will have His glo-ry on us. We will have His glo-ry on us.

We will have His glo-ry on us when He's through.

ANCHORED IN THE OCEANS

And if one prevail against him, two shall withstand him; and A THREE-FOLD CORD is not quickly broken. Ecclesiastes 4:12

God is throwing out a lifeline to anchor us. It is a threefold cord: prayer, praise and the power of His Word. All three elements of believers' lives must remain intertwined, to keep an open Heaven above them.

Without praise and worship, it is difficult to enter into the realm of the Spirit of God.

Enter into his gates with thanksgiving, and into his courts with praise: be thankful unto him, and bless his name. For the LORD is good; his mercy is everlasting; and his truth endureth to all generations. Psalm 100:4-5

Without the Spirit, prayer is a dry and formal drudgery, a hopeless venture at best. But when Heaven is open, the Master's voice is inviting and the Holy Spirit is leading, prayer becomes an unending adventure.

Without power, the Word of God is only the letter of the Law that kills. But when it is studied, read or preached with reverence for God's integrity and seen as a covenant-binding contract of promise that He longs to fulfill with His *Oceans of Glory*, then it generates expectancy for revelation and power that brings miracles to pass.

The Word of God judges the good or bad fruits of all spiritual manifestations. The Spirit and the Word must agree. Still, I have heard some tell me that in the laughing revival, they had no time for the Word. Pastors reported that members booed when they began to minister in a teaching mode to instill godly principles for Christian living — *"line upon line and precept upon precept."*

The Word of God judges the good or bad fruits of all spiritual manifestations.

PRAYER

Still others told me that "travail" was no longer necessary as a form of prayer. I watched some of these fall into disaster, not able to recover their ministries. The early Church was far more advanced in the spirit of revival than we have yet to comprehend, and if they needed prayer warriors, then so do we. So great was their witness of signs, wonders and convicting words, that persecution caused the martyrdom of many of them. This was not a mark of weakness. Peter was indebted to a group of people who prayed him out of prison.

> *My little children, of whom I travail in birth again until Christ be formed*
> *in you ...* Galatians 4:19

If revival is about souls, then how can we say that travail need no longer be practiced or taught? Do not new converts need Christ formed within them? Granted, when you have, indeed, broken through the veil of flesh into a heavenly-throne-room experience, you will experience more grace and less agony in prayer. And we certainly do not need to imitate excessive movements, sounds and gestures that others have made in the agony of prayers of travail, unless we are truly being inspired by the Spirit of God to do so.

How foolish it would be for the friend of a pregnant woman to accompany her to the birthing room, lie down on a gurney next to her and imitate the agony of childbirth! No, she may be needed to midwife or add a comforting hand of strength to the lady in delivery, but she cannot travail for her.

A threefold cord is not easily broken: prayer, praise and the power of the Word of God. Practicing all three will keep the Church in balance, and our lives full of sweetness and power.

 It is a threefold cord: prayer, praise and the power of the Word of God.

On February 19, 2000, I instantly changed some travel plans, to fly to Bob Shattles' meetings at White Horse Christian Center in West Lafayette, Indiana. [1] The Holy Spirit showed me to change my calendar and not miss those days of meetings. He instructed me not to be distracted on the Monday of that weekend. I was to come to the church sanctuary and pray, no matter what I might encounter in the way of offers to fellowship and the like. "You have an appoint-ment for an audience with Me," the Lord told me. I obeyed.

On that Sunday night, we had a tremendous soul-winning meeting. More than a hundred young people received Christ or rededicated their lives to Him, and Brother Bob worked the prayer lines until one o'clock in the morning. It was hard to get up early the next morning when my ride woke me to go to the church.

Upon arriving, I met Barb, one of the staff. She came in shortly to clean the sanctuary with the vacuum cleaner. When she realized that I was actually there to pray, she said, "Oh, Sister Shelli, you won't be able to hear yourself think with this vacuum cleaner running. Last night, the unchurched came, and they left the place looking like a movie theater. Now that's revival, but it will take us all day to clean up." Barb was genuinely excited, rejoicing in what it symbol-ized. However, she was concerned about me being disappointed in my effort to pray. So, she assured me that I was welcome to stay as she went on to clean.

I started to walk away, but then my heart was quickened: "Revival is never convenient. It is just something you *must* do. Some people are scheduled so tightly in their activities that they would have to schedule God to get revived." I had used that statement many times of late in my preaching, and I was finding that God rarely moves when He is unwelcome because of our tight schedules. But that morning He himself had scheduled me for a divine appointment there at that altar, a place on the platform stairs where the youth group had placed a great wooden cross upon the steps with flowers.

I turned back to Barb and rejoiced with her. "That's okay. Don't worry about me. I'll be just fine ... if it is no bother." She assured me that it was no problem and went on to clean, as I went to pray.

Then the devil whispered to me; "Ha! Aren't you the Pharisee this morning? Praying like this out in the open so everyone will know that you came here to pray!" For an instant, I thought it was the Holy Ghost rebuking me for some-thing I mistakenly had thought He told me to do there, and I started to walk away. But no sooner had I neared the door than I realized it wasn't the Lord's voice at all.

No! I had not taken time out of my schedule just to fly in and show off. This was not a matter of pride. God had inspired my heart to meet Him at that altar, and normally the sanctuary was very quiet at that time of day. I had done noth-ing wrong, and when I realized it, I went back to the altar in a hurry. We have to press in to the things of God. It was a pure-hearted plan, and that was a critical factor in what was about to happen. Motives are important.

Blessed are the pure in heart, for they will see God.

Matthew 5:8, NIV

It is only right for us to judge our heart in a situation like this, but if it condemns us not, if everyone is willing to accommodate our plan and we are able to honor those in charge, we may proceed.

When I did, at last, settle in to pray that day, weariness from my back-to-back meeting schedule and travel overtook me. I heard the vacuum cleaner begin to roar, and Barb had been right — I could not hear myself think. A plan began to settle in upon my flesh: "Ah! Sleep! No one will ever know. You can pray when you wake up!"

I started to nod off saying the name of Jesus. Then, suddenly, there was a swish of blue fabric out of the peripheral vision of my right eye. Someone was standing at the pulpit on the platform above the cross. I thought it was Barb, coming to clean there or to tell me something. Startled, I looked up, only to find that it was Jesus.

Never in my entire life had I thought of seeing Him in broad daylight with my eyes wide open. I had seen Him in dreams or visions of the night, and even been carried away to Heaven in an out-of-body experience twice, but all of that had happened with my eyes closed. Yet, here He was, very unexpectedly, unannounced, there at the altar to speak to me a message about His Church. I was in shock.

The Lord was standing there in a royal-bluish-purple satin robe of many rich folds. Over His shoulder was a deep-cranberry satin traveling cloak, or mantle. It was embroidered all over with gold thread and then covered with a fine gold dusting that shimmered on the surface of the fabric.

Jesus was staring at me, waiting for me to notice Him. Had I slept, I would never have known He was there watching me. When I looked up, He spoke.

His voice did not touch my ears, but rang into my heart: "This church has pressed in to such a place in Me, through their prayers and worship and servant's heart, that I will now be able to dwell with them on a much more tangible level."

Then the Lord vanished. His message had been short and sweet and to the point. I went to tell Pastors Johns and Shattles what I had experienced, and we all rejoiced together. That night, in the evening service, there was more.

PRAISE

The praise and worship that evening went on for over an hour, until people left their seats and began spontaneously to dance all over the front of the church. Pastor Shattles and I were sitting on the front row when the worship service began. I had on a lovely black suit, and so did he. Suddenly, we looked down about waist high between our seats, and a sifting of fine "dust" of a golden rain was swirling between our chairs. It was light-filled, and it landed on the floor, on our hands and on our suits. It tickled us like children. We sensed that God was going to reveal Himself in signs and wonders that night, and indeed, later in the services, He did. A boy who had not walked in nine years was able to get up from his wheelchair alone and stand, and more than fifty teenagers were saved.

I looked up to see if the pastor had noticed what was occurring. I thought that he must be the tall figure standing on the platform directly in front of me, but he had not yet entered the sanctuary. That tall figure was the Lord again, just as in the morning.

There Jesus stood, three-dimensional, right in front of me. It had now happened twice in less than twenty-four hours. What was this all about? I was amazed and stunned.

The Lord told me to watch carefully, and He began to pull on what appeared to be a large rope. It was the kind used to tie calves with, to secure the stakes of a tent or to set the sail of a tall ship or its anchor. He tugged on it three times hard, and on the third tug, a flap of canvas swirled past me and then, beneath it, attached to the rope, was a tent stake.

Jesus spoke again, "I am pulling up the tent stakes. Out with the old! Up with the new! The cloud is moving; move with the cloud!"

Then He vanished. No one else had seen Him.

As I thought on what the Lord had said, I was reminded of a sermon by Dr. Lester Sumrall preached at Pastor Jess Gibson's church in Springfield, Missouri. Dr. Sumrall was one of God's true generals, and before he died, we heard him say that God had kept him current in every wave of successive outpourings of the glory in his lifetime. He had not bound himself to only one, nor had he missed any. "When the Spirit is moving left," he said, "go left. When He is moving right, go right. Catch the next wave and ride it."

Jesus was letting me know that change might not be easy, but, in obedience, I had better prepare for it and obey. I turned to Bob and said, "There is Jesus again!"

"Where?" he asked, looking around. But the Lord had already gone.

I told Bob what had happened, then I got so excited that I jumped up among the young people, who were dancing in the Spirit in the front of the platform, and danced all over that area. As I twirled, several people in the back came forward and began to pat my shoulder. I did not know why at the time. Later, they testified, "Did you know that there was a cloud of golden dust over your head raining down your back? It was following you, or you were following it."

I had not told anyone but Bob that Jesus had appeared to me or that He had said: "The cloud is moving; move with the cloud." How wonderful that He confirmed it in this way!

"I am pulling up the tent stakes. Out with the old! Up with the new! The cloud is moving; move with the cloud!"

As I danced, my hands began to burn with a fire as hot as a stove. The unction to lay hands on ninety-two-year-old Mama Jenkins came upon me. She had traveled all day on a bus, from the funeral of our friends Linda and Joe Knight, to be there in the services with us. She was tired, and her ankles were swollen. When I bent over and laid hands on them, they were instantly healed.

Standing back up, I suddenly felt as though the glory of the Lord had surrounded me tighter than being packed in styrofoam. I could not move, and could barely breathe. This resulted in being slain in the Spirit on the floor next to her chair. Mama later told us that she, too, had seen Jesus standing there. Hmm...

His presence was tangible that night in the church, just as He had said in the morning to me at the altar.

While I was there on the floor, I saw the Lord again, for the third time that day; only this time my eyes were completely closed. He was not talking, but seemed to be waiting for a response from me. Finally I asked him, "Lord, if the cloud is moving and we are to move with the cloud, would you mind telling me what *is* the cloud?"

He said, "Whereas, in the history of the Church, healing has been in the hands of but a few, it now passes to the hands of many. Teach them and release them, and great shall be the multiplication of signs and wonders and of healing miracles in the Church in this generation."

I understood that a great wave of healing would follow a great move of prayer. More direction for following the road map of revival had come.

I understood that a great wave of healing would follow a great move of prayer.

THE WORD OF GOD

I also understood what it was that I was to teach the people. Many need to listen to the healing scriptures on tape and read them aloud every day. We can become weak in our faith because we do not have a knowledge of what God has promised to do for us. Even if we receive our miracles, the devil comes to steal them right away, and some give in, out of ignorance. We must fight the good fight of faith to hold onto every inch of territory the Lord has promised to us.

How do we fight? Find a promise of God in His Word and put Him in remembrance of it through prayer and the confession of that promise. Then praise Him for the victory until it manifests.

Put me in remembrance: let us plead together: declare thou, that thou mayest be justified.   Isaiah 43:26

In Minneapolis, a few years ago, in the church of Pastors Lynn and Mac Hammond, Living Word Christian Center of Brooklyn Park, I heard a testimony about a father who had believed God for a creative miracle for his baby, yet in his wife's womb. Janice Walker's pregnancy had been diagnosed as a fetus with a terminal defect, possibly without a brain. Doctors recommended abortion and assured her and Mark that the child either would be born dead or would die at birth. But Mark knew God could change all of that. He took the healing scriptures to work with him, and on breaks he sat and fasted meals, and spoke them out loud over his developing child. There is no distance in the Spirit, and Mark believed that God could hear him. [2]

At home, he would intensely continue this regime, laying hands on his wife's belly, and the two of them together would call those things that be not as though they were. Finally, the child, a little girl, Elizabeth, was born. She had a brain after all, although it was only one-fourth the size of the normal brain. Whether in the womb or out, her development made no difference to the believing father, who continued the regime faithfully, rejoicing in God. When the child was tested at the age of two, her brain had increased to three-quarters normal size —a medical miracle.

At age three, the child had a desire to play the piano. Her mother told me that she heard the little girl praying about it and felt the tangible presence of the Lord fill the atmosphere. Three weeks later, an unexpected gift of a spinet piano was given for Elizabeth, a little life with a purpose. She did not sink in the oceans of adversity; she lives and plays in the *Oceans of Glory!* [3]

I teach people everywhere I go to call those things that be not as though they were. In my services, I call four people up to participate in an illustration. They each represent a "kidney," in its north, south, east and west parts. Then I send them each to stand at a different exit. The congregation can see that the parts of that kidney are still in the room, but it is no longer as easy to discern the whole. The parts are all spread out.

Then I make the "four parts" disappear out the exit doors, and I tell them to come back when they hear us calling out, "Kidney, come!" The congregation helps me to call, and when we do, the parts of the kidney, represented by those four people, all come running back into the sanctuary.

They never all arrive at the same time. Usually the folks in the audience are laughing by the time the slowest one comes huffing and puffing to the front to rejoin the other three representatives in my illustrated sermon.

Then I am able to encourage the people: "See! Patience and faith paid off. We knew they would come! We just had to wait for them." This is how I get the people to extend their faith for creative miracles. The particles and parts are there when the atmosphere is charged with healing. We have to work with the Spirit of God and not get in a hurry. We have to patiently and unrelentlessly call the things that be not as though they were into our three-dimensional realm.

This is how I have been able to pray for so many people to receive new knee joints recently. Some of those miracles took fifteen or twenty minutes at the altar, and during that time everyone else waited.

On February 18, in Tulsa, Oklahoma, a woman who participated as one of my volunteers in the "kidney" illustration was the last one of the four people that I chose to come back to the front of the auditorium. Later, at the end of the service, she came up for prayer for a blind eye. I had never experienced a blind eye opening in my ministry, although I myself had been healed of astigmatism and of the need for bifocals when I was just eighteen.

Before I prayed for the woman, who told us that her optic nerve was dried up, I said, "You will receive it, if you stay in faith, even as we waited for you to come forth in the 'kidney' illustration."

She was thrilled, and allowed us to pray and say, "Eye see! Sight come, in the name of Jesus!" Over and over, we said it together with all the audience, with commanding faith. Her vision slowly returned. Eventually, I asked an usher to bring an unfamiliar book with fine print to her. She left, able to read it with her good eye covered.

 Whereas in the history of the Church, healing has been in the hands of but a few, it now passes to the hands of many. Teach them and release them, and great shall be the multiplication of signs and wonders and of healing miracles in the Church in this generation.

In services in Maine, we saw the audience, night after night, receive like this. I would stop in the middle of telling about the open vision of Jesus and ask them all to look down at their hands. "Do you see anything about your hands that would be something you did not ever notice before? Healing passes to the hands of many." Many — laughing, weeping, shaking, shouting or silently — raised their hands. I would tell them, "Good, just keep checking them out," and I finished my sermon.

After I finished preaching, I called the people up front and interviewed them.

Some had oil beading up on their palms and fingers. Some had a glowing amber gold-colored "dust," fine and minute, popping through the pores of their skin. Sometimes it was mixed with oil. Sometimes there was much, and sometimes only a speck or two.

This has continued until this time. Sometimes the substance on the people's hands is like an emerald or sapphire in color. It is a miracle anointing forming in their hands. Sometimes, their hands feel hot.

We never focus on the signs until the preaching of the Word has been honored first. At that point, I say to the congregation, "Who needs a miracle?" The ones who raise their hands are called to the front. Then I station them in front of those who are holding out their hands full of miracle anointing, and I tell those who have come for miracles, "The strongest anointing in the house tonight is right here on these hands. God did this, and it is sovereign. Let us receive from the vessels He has chosen tonight."

As the ministry of healing passes into the hands of many, we have been seeing many healings. We enjoy sitting back and watching the Body ministry released like this. People get so excited that they forget that I am in the building, and that is wonderful! Jesus is the one who is being glorified. Hallelujah!

The power of the praise service and the preaching of the Word of God brings the signs and directs people to the Source, Jesus, and gives instruction as to how to apply the threefold cord to anchor them for their miracles. Goosebumps are of no use without direction and instruction, but if people are taught to reverence God and look for a useful application of the signs and wonders for the healing of bodies or the winning of souls, it is good.

What good would it do to turn on a water faucet for a drink and forget a cup? What a waste of the outpouring! What good would it do to send an ocean liner into the ocean with no compass or navigational chart? Prayer is the portal that opens up for oceans to pour through. Praise is the hoist of the anchor that keeps the ship in the place where the blessings abide. And the Word of God is the navigational system that directs the power to fuel a successful journey in such deep water — the anointing. Without it, the flood will not bless you, but destroy you.

- **Prayer is the portal.**
- **Praise is the hoist of the anchor.**
- **The Word of God is the navigational system.**

That reminds me of a story I heard Rev. Benny Hinn telling on TBN television a few years ago. He was supposed to be getting dressed in his hotel room to go lay hands on thousands of people in one of his crusades. Instead of being able to dress, however, he was so ill with flu symptoms that he could barely stand up. He cried out to the Lord to help him. When the Lord answered him, it didn't sound very spiritual, and at first, he ignored it or discounted the answer.

God had said to his heart, "Benny, turn on the television." Was the Lord trying to tell him to stay in the room and cancel the service? He didn't think so. But that answer seemed silly when such an important issue as being healed in order to help bring healing to others was at stake. Again the Holy Spirit told his heart, "Go turn on the television." So at last, he obeyed. When the screen cleared, to his surprise, the image staring back at him was none other than his own (prerecorded in another crusade).

The Benny Hinn on television was well and ministering under the anointing. He told the viewing audience to lay their hands on the television set and catch the anointing that was upon the service. But the Benny Hinn in the hotel room said, "God, You've got to be kidding! That's me on TV."

As I recall, the Lord answered him this way: "Yes, that is Benny Hinn with the anointing, and you are Benny Hinn with the flu. Lay your hands on the television set as I commanded him to say, and you will be healed." Benny did just that and was healed instantly and went to minister to the hurting people in his crusade.

It's wonderful to have the anointing, but that is as the Holy Spirit wills, and so when you are not particularly anointed or around a special gift of healing in operation, it is so good to also be able to get healed by faith — even if you are Benny Hinn healing Benny Hinn. We must realize that without the anointing upon us, even those who are called in fivefold ministry have to live by faith. *"The just shall live by faith!"*

I love that story. We must be led of the Spirit. Faith, hope and love ... the anchor holds. Let us not be disheartened or slack in our spiritual stance, but press in and become firmly anchored in God's *Oceans of Glory*.

ENDNOTE

1. You can watch their live services from a link off our website: http://members.aol.com/shellibake/index.html.
2. "Living Proof" by Melanie Henry, *Living Words* magazine (Minneapolis, MN: 1994).
3. Watch this testimony of a medical miracle on video: *Real People, Real Needs, Real Victories*, Kenneth Copeland Ministries (Fort Worth, TX). The video can be ordered from their website.

DRAWN OUT OF THE WATERS

He sent from above, he took me, he drew me out of many waters.
Psalm 18:16

And she called his name Moses: and she said, Because I drew him out of the water.
Exodus 2:10

And were all baptized unto Moses in the cloud and in the sea; and did all eat the same spiritual meat; and did all drink the same spiritual drink: for they drank of that spiritual Rock that followed them: and that Rock was Christ. But with many of them God was not well pleased: for they were overthrown in the wilderness.
1 Corinthians 10:2-5

God drew Moses out of the waters of chaos and adversity. Prophetically, he became a symbol of God's insatiable desire to rescue man from life's dark, stormy waters. *"Deep calleth unto deep,"* as God's Spirit perpetually searches the seas of men for one who will answer the call. He needs many deliverers like Moses (whose name, *Moshe,* in Hebrew actually means "the drawn-out one").

DRAWN OUT

The towns around the Sea of Galilee contained the deliverers whom Jesus needed in His ministry, fishermen with names like Peter, James and John, drawn out of their fishing boats to become fishers of men. Seventy more were chosen for lesser tasks, but apparently most of them fled, not able to endure the firmness of the teachings or the rigors of the journey and the storms of persecution (see Luke 10:1).

Unto those who were faithful to the call, the Lord returned the favor and rescued them from the storms at sea. His heart grieved over those who would not follow, because He needed their assistance. He once said, *"For many are called, but few are chosen"* (Matthew 22:14). He would have delivered them all through the same waters.

Through the waters of the Red Sea, God delivered more than a million of Moses' followers. All of them endured the challenge and witnessed the miracles, but God was not pleased with those who drew back rather than continuing to be "drawn out," out into greater depths of victory and testimony. They were responsible for what they experienced. *"Unto whomsoever much is given, of him shall much be required"* (Luke 12:48).

They saw the water of the Red Sea congeal to rescue them. The glory made the water congeal (meaning "to freeze into ice," "crystallize" or "gel"). [1] It parted and became as if it was two huge rolled-back walls of ice in the hot desert climate of the Middle East. In this simple illustration, we can at least attempt to understand a supernatural miracle: the molecular structure of an object changing from one substance to another, just as water congeals to ice and melts again (see Exodus 15:8).

This is the same thing that happened to some objects in the Bible: a metal ax head that floated, water that turned into wine, five loaves and two fish that fed five thousand, the skins of lepers that became whole, an almond rod that budded, men who walked on water and dead who were raised. In modern times, we personally know of ministers who have had water turn to gasoline, empty flour bins that fed families, and money that has multiplied in wallets and in pockets. How do these things happen? They are changed in the glory.

The Israelites did not pass on dry land through a "nothing," or a "void," in between those two walls of congealed water (see Psalm 78:13). No, they passed through a "something" that held it back, the *Oceans of Glory*, greater in weight and size than that tiny Red Sea! A full container of water will be displaced when a greater force pours into it. Hallelujah! When the enemy comes in like a flood, the Lord raises up a standard against him. Why? Because He is an ocean.

When the last Israelite passed safely to the other side, the glory departed with him, and, in the absence of the glory, the waters melted back together and overflowed the armies of Pharaoh, killing them all. Oh, to be on the hot fire side of God's glory, rather than on the backside of ice! To be in His favor and blessing, rather than in His judgments!

The children of Israel were all "Moshes" that day — people "drawn out of water," just like their deliverer Moses. After that, God saw them as equal to Moses and invited them to come up to the mountain, for all had been baptized with the same waters and glory fire, as they passed together through the *Oceans of Glory.*

But the people didn't see themselves that way. Too terrified of the "supernatural," a power that could literally change one substance into another, they dreaded going up the mountain to the next level, saying, "No, Moses, you go without us!" (see Deuteronomy 5:27). God had to let them fall behind, as they refused to follow Him. How heartbreaking to watch them drown in the seas of adversity in the midst of a dry desert *where no water was* after they had been miraculously "drawn out" of the water of the Red Sea!

We are a people of the late 1990s era of "laughing" revivals and massive "repentance" revivals of Toronto and Brownsville, and we have entered the 2000s in vast wonder at what lies before us. Should God once more repeat His revival cycles and visit us with *Oceans of Glory*, we will be forever responsible. Will we only "play" in the river and romp in the ocean's foamy edge for ourselves, or we will go to the next level — "drawn out" as deliverers for our time?

What an awesome responsibility to be among the people whom God has called to lay hands upon the sick and watch them recover, to pray for nations to be discipled, to be His witnesses in all the earth! Covet His blessings, that we may hear the word "Well done, good and faithful servants" on Judgment Day.

Only be careful, and watch yourselves closely so that you do not forget the things your eyes have seen or let them slip from your heart as long as you live. TEACH THEM TO YOUR CHILDREN AND TO THEIR CHILDREN AFTER THEM. Deuteronomy 4:9, NIV

 Will we only "play" in the river and romp in the ocean's foamy edge for ourselves, or we will go to the next level — "drawn out" as deliverers for our time?

Oceans of Glory rumble in the near distance, as the forerunner waves have already begun to announce their coming. What will we do to prepare? Are we praying? Are we praising? Are we meditating on the Word of God? He is calling for all who will ready themselves.

If you have to go to the mountain alone, will you go? Sometimes, others may not want to take the limits off of God in their thinking in order to experience His limitless depths. Be full of courage! You may have to be like the brave little frog that I heard about. He fell into a vat of cream with some buddies one day, as they were playing leapfrog. It had been a happy game until that moment.

"Alas," his buddies cried, "We shall drown! The top is too high to reach!"

But the little frog kept paddling. "No, it isn't," he said. "I believe someone will come to 'draw us out.' "

The others soon drowned in frantic fear, but the little frog paddled until the liquid cream turned to solid butter, and he was then able to jump to the top and escape.

Oceans of Glory

An Audience With God

The Holy Spirit is searching the seas of people in our generation to draw out new miracle workers: pastors, teachers, apostles, evangelists and prophets, to network together. He offers an audience with instruction, if we have the patience to be drawn aside and listen. Such an experience, in 1980, changed my entire life and prepared me for this creative miracle ministry flow today.

I had sold all my earthly possessions in Plymouth, Massachusetts, put my art career on hold, and traveled west to attend Bible school. My first stop was the great Campmeeting of Kenneth Hagin. Kenneth Copeland, a guest minister, was there preaching about the light and the glory. I had come too far to be deterred from receiving every last drop of what God had to pour into my life that day. As the worship team finished the service, I got stuck in that place of praise. Since then, I have gotten stuck in a lot places of praise as services were closing. It is becoming increasingly difficult for me to leave buildings on time.

We will soon come to the place that our buildings of worship will not close. The glory will be felt twenty-four hours a day. Some will get off work from the night shift, come into the glory and be able to go back to work in the morning. That's the way the coal miners were revived in Wales. Those who worked the night shift would greet the men of the morning shift, who were singing hymns of the services they had attended all night long. That joyful witness drew the night shift into the same services.

After Brother Copeland finished his sermon, some friends asked me to go get a hot dog for lunch, but I couldn't move. My hands remained straight up in the air, as they had been in worship. This was not greatly appreciated, and some people grumbled about my blocking the exit for an entire row.

I finally managed to move my knees, and again I heard, "Let's go get a hot dog." About that time, I also heard a thunderous sound, as if the northeast corner of the civic center had just been torn off by an explosion. A great sucking force seemed to be pulling me up, and I heard the Holy Spirit saying, "Come up higher. Behold the reward of the prophets, the priests and the kings."

I heard Him say it three times, although my friends hadn't heard or felt anything. They were still saying, "Let's go get a hot dog," but I was hearing from God Almighty and feeling my spirit being drawn out to the very edge of my body. It was pulling me out into the glory, as they, in the carnal realm, kept saying, "Let's go get a hot dog!"

 Come up higher. Behold the reward of prophets, the priests and the kings.

We all need to be very sensitive when we are leaving services that God has visited. It is important not to yank people out of a critical place in God that they may have come to in the closing moments of the meeting. They may have received a decisive life-changing word. I had sold all of my earthly possessions and traveled two thousand miles to get to that civic center, and now that I had heard that word from God, who cared about a silly hot dog? I had come for an audience with God, and He was inviting me to go higher.

 We all need to be very sensitive when we are leaving services that God has visited.

I do not like to see ushers pull anyone up off the floor who may have been slain in the Spirit. Nor do I think that intercessors or others should attempt to fan the flame over them or touch them or speak to them unless prompted by God. Realize that in such a state of being, those individuals, doing "carpet duty," are possibly in a higher and better place than anyone else on earth at that moment, if they are fully caught away in the glory realm. What could anyone who is still alert in the earthly realm possibly offer them?

How foolish to interfere with what God is doing! Many may be floundering through life because we have not allowed them to have such an audience with God, because some carnal person only cared about feeding his flesh a hot dog!

In the end, I felt a little folded-up note drop into my lap and a friendly tap on my shoulder, and my friends said, "That's okay, honey. We see that you are caught in a place with God," and they left.

I thought, *You got that right.* What a shame they didn't want to stay there and pray with me!

Commissioned for Ministry

As I stayed in the presence of God, He pulled me up, and I saw the harvest and received a more specific call to the ministry, with instructions that later proved critical to success. Then Jesus took me to a place where He stood in front of a man who was missing a right arm. His good arm was stretched out on his left side. I stood there looking at that young man, about eighteen to twenty years old. It puzzled me. Jesus had just shown me the harvest. I thought, *What's this all about?*

Then Jesus was standing there. He said, "I command you to receive creative miracles."

I choked, "You what? You mean You're not asking me?"

I could not believe what the heavenly Bridegroom was saying to me. We love to boast about being His Bride, but we don't like to obey Him sometimes. You would think that a person would be more sensible than to say no to Jesus in

Heaven, but I did it. I was foolish and ignorant and made out of flesh, and I stood there and said, "Lord, You know that I can receive this up here. But my body is sitting back down there in that auditorium on earth, and I have a funny feeling that You are going to send me back there shortly. We're in a different realm here, but when I get back down to that three-dimensional realm, You know we're going to have trouble with this."

The Lord didn't show me even an ounce of compassion. An English evangelist that I know once said, "You have to wake people up to the state of mind they are in with forceful action." Jesus did not show ooey-gooey time-wasting emotion on Peter during that storm on the water. He gave him one chance, and spoke to him straightforwardly: "Walk."

A.A. Allen, a famous healing evangelist of the 1940s, was reported to have taken a child with deformed legs who walked like a monkey and thrust him across the stage toward his mother. How shocked she was to see the child running toward her, when she had supposed he would have fallen down injured. You had better not do anything like that if Jesus didn't tell you to do it. You had better know that you know that you know that you know in your knower! Be sure, or you may spend the rest of your life in jail.

That English evangelist told me about one of his recent services where he was led to tell a woman to take off her neck brace. She was very fearful and resisted the idea completely, even though she had come willingly into the healing line. Finally, he told her that he was going to tear it off if she did not, for he felt that though the woman had consulted God to heal her, her resistance was now a mockery. Finally, she took it off herself, and she was healed. Later, he learned that her injury had been so severe that her back would have collapsed if she had not been truly healed of God.

 You had better not do anything like that if Jesus didn't tell you to do it.

Imagine Moses leading the fearful children of Israel into their miracle, as they stared at water rolling back into two huge walls as firm as ice and heard the beating hoofs of Pharaoh's armies behind them. We must not judge those of ancient times and wonder why they resisted God. If you were the lady in the neck brace or the mother of the "monkey" child, how would you have reacted?

Our "Christian" society likes to make the Bible and Jesus so "cutsey" and sweet. We put little cherubs on Bible totes and fake smiles on in abundance sometimes, and we like to glamorize things. But the Bible is actually a very bloody book, and it says very clearly: *"It is a fearful thing to fall into the hands of the living God"* (Hebrews 10:31). Why is this true? Because He is a consuming fire! He is also an ocean, and I surely wouldn't want to fall into that without a life preserver. Would you?

Praise God for the blood Of Jesus. Some would say, "But these are New Testament times." Yes, they are. Did you ever study the words of rebuke to the seven churches in the book of Revelation? Peace comes from being in harmony with God.

My Jesus is very strong. You can sense that in what He said to me — "I command you to receive creative miracles." That's all the answer He gave me.

I said, "All right. How does it work?"

He said, "In the hour that your knowledge becomes full, so will your faith." That was 1980, and since then I have been meditating on the how, where, why and when. Just because Jesus said to me," I command you to receive," did not guarantee that I would do it. He told the entire Body of Christ to win souls, and not many have. When we are commissioned to do something far beyond our level of faith, we must meditate on it, worship God and seek Him until the anointing for it comes. When we seek Him with all of our hearts, we have the promise that *"all these things shall be added unto you"* (Matthew 6:33).

 In the hour that your knowledge becomes full, so will your faith.

"I command you to receive creative miracles." What did it mean? I could sense the Holy Spirit joining in on that conversation: "You'd better get busy finding out how to know, because I'm going to hold you responsible when you come up here at the end of your life."

My honest reaction was, "I wish I hadn't come, because I do not want to deal with this puzzle. This is challenging me too much, Jesus."

But I knew that it was too late. *"To whom much is given, much is required."* There is a great responsibility in touching the glory of Heaven. I knew that when I allowed God to take me into that visitation. After the friends stopped inviting me to eat a hot dog, there still remained a barrier to the release of my spirit. It was even greater than their peer pressure. It was my own fear of what the call might signify. My earthly goals were not very important to the Lord in the scope of eternity. He was looking for a soul-winner, a laborer. He had wept when He was on earth because He found so few.

How To Receive Miracles

After I accepted the command to take creative miracles into my ministry, I asked, "How?"

The Lord answered me with a physics lesson, although I had no such degree. He will not lead you without provision. "To Me, natural and supernatural are all one realm," He said. "To man, they are separate; to Me, there is no separation between the two realms. I am more scientific than science. Science will never figure Me out." [2]

He will not lead you without provision.

The Lord went on: "I operate at a higher realm of glory and light than that of earthly light" (which moves at 186,300 miles per second). "I am light, and light comes from Me. No one will ever calculate My speed."

> *The true light that gives light to every man was coming into the world.*
> *He was in the world, and though the world was made through him, the world*
> *did not recognize him.*   John 1:9-11, NIV

I said, "How so?"

The Lord said, "Behold, the blast of a nuclear bomb," and at that instant, I saw one, brighter than the noonday sun. It was as if we had flown to the other side of the world and watched it.

"Look at that," He said, and in a split atomic second, there was a burst of light and a wedge carved into the universe. The burst of light traveled at a higher atomic speed than 186,300 miles per second, and as the energy of the blast and the light produced from it wound down to a slower earthly speed and could be perceived, it created a substance that had the power to bring life, or it had the power to bring death — fallout. [3]

Jesus said, "When the Father spoke, it was on a sound wave. He hovered over the darkness and said, 'Light be,' and there was light. When He speaks creative miracles out of the realm of Heaven, they come forth. When they come forth, they travel at high speeds of light toward earth. And as they break through the earth's atmosphere, where you live in the three-dimensional realm, they begin to unwind in the revolutions of their speed and become denser, forming matter, a perceivable substance that you can see, touch and feel. Each one of those glory-filled sounds has a code in it, a boundary to it, like the oceans My Father has set."

When God speaks forth a "kidney," then it will not defy that coded structure and become an arm. And as that glory-filled sound wave winds down to its coded atomic speed limit and boundary, substance is formed." [4] Every atom, every cell and every element — vegetable, mineral or otherwise — has a set and fixed boundary established by the Word of God. The electrons and protons in each atom obey the positive and negative charges and revolve around the nucleus at speeds preset by God's ordinance or covenant boundaries. These laws cannot be superseded — unless He intervenes:

> *He forgave us all our sins, HAVING CANCELED THE WRITTEN CODE,*
> *with its regulations, that was against us and that stood opposed to us; he took*
> *it away, nailing it to the cross.*   Colossians 2:13-14, NIV [5]

We know that the context of this scripture also includes the legal codes of the Torah, the Law that restricted the Jewish population from sin and Gentile transgressions. God has set boundaries for all of life to obey Him, for divine order and excellence in the glory:

> *Thus saith the* LORD; *If my covenant be not with day and night, and if I have not appointed the ordinances of heaven and earth ...* Jeremiah 33:25

There is a higher realm than that of light, a realm of divine thought. Angels hearken to the thoughts of God, which travel faster than light. It is the consciousness of who He is.

In the moment that a thought of pride and rebellion was found in Lucifer, he was cast down as a lightning bolt. The Bible says he fell like a morning star (at the speed of light). The thought was faster than the lightning that followed.

Jesus told me that He would give me an answer that would even fascinate space scientists, whom I would talk to someday. Sure enough, it happened — seven years later in Houston, Texas. They said, "Little lady, you don't have a physics degree. Where did you get that?"

I answered, "Talking to God in the Holy Ghost" (see 1 Corinthians 14:2). Many of them understood, and some of the most brilliant among them told me that they had finalized their answers to complicated physics questions, not behind their desks, but on their knees. Of course, you will not read *that* in your science or history books.

Jesus continued with my lesson on creative miracles, "Uranium is the densest matter that you know of on the face of the earth." (That made me think that maybe there are more elements that we don't yet know about.) "The sound revolutions," the Lord continued, "and the speed of the level of light traveling on the inside of each nucleus of each atom of each molecule inside of uranium is a whole lot slower (denser) than that which circulates in air.[6] But it is so compacted that when you cause the fission process to take place, it explodes in an atomic second, in a burst of light, as in a nuclear explosion. These are the formulas behind creation and resurrection that man does not yet fully comprehend or know how to function in."

Then the Lord showed me how a creative miracle took place. There needed to be a wedge of time and space expanded into a current situation to insert the missing part and interrupt the realm of physics that we operate in down here on earth. A glory-filled declarative voice with a gift of faith can do this, much as one would drive a wedge into a log of wood. Then the Lord showed me how God expands the atmosphere to bring forth molecules and particles that we do not perceive because they are not solid or tightly bound in such a way that we can perceive them. Nevertheless, they are always present, as He is.

He showed me the body of Adam, and it was very large. In my vision, it was difficult to perceive Adam, for he was so full of glory, and it expanded him inside and out. He glowed, as Jesus must have on the Mount of Transfiguration. Liquid light flowed through Adam's veins, and he was almost transparent. Still, he maintained a true bodily, earthly form.

Then I saw the glory flee from him in an instant, and he became much darker, a mere shadow of the man he once was. He was instantly smaller in size and fearfully aware of the environment that towered over him, which only moments before, he had dominated. The Lord showed me that when the glory fled from Adam's veins, his life source, blood, was weakened and missing key elements that glory had once provided. His DNA was damaged by this loss and couldn't reproduce healthy descendants, of the same original level he had once lived in.

Then the Lord showed me how He and the angels could exist with all of Heaven in a realm right inside of ours, or vice versa. I saw how they could appear and disappear at the will of God. He *draws them out* at will. This should be explained in childlike terms. Things should be simple, even mathematics and science, but I never understood them until the genius of the Holy Ghost flooded my soul, and I began to pray out mysteries in tongues. Now, I enjoy both math and science immensely. It will be great fun to one day explore the universe with the Creator. What a tour guide He will be! And what a tour!

A Simple Illustration: "Connect the Dots"

1. Hold out your hand. If you have a ring on, take it off and place it in your palm. Let the space inside that ring represent the four corners of Adam: his north, south, east and west parts (or, if you prefer, his top, bottom, left side and right side).
2. With a pen, place four dots inside of that circle to represent all of that. Notice how the ring dominates the substance of those four points. Can you see how Adam dominated his world?
3. Now, remove the ring. Take away the container, the organizer of the dots. Take away the crown of dominion that the gold ring could symbolize over those dots of earthly substance. Scatter the dots.
4. Now, erase the dots and redraw them on the four corners of your palm, two on either side of your wrist and two on either side of your palm under the index finger and the little finger. You can still see the dots, but now they are spread apart.
5. Now, erase them again. Go to the four corners of the room. Put a dot in each corner and come back to the center of the room. You know those dots are there, but it is now very difficult to discern them.

6. Now, put a dot in each of the four corners of your yard and walk back inside the house. Can you perceive them at all? Of course not. Actually, however, they are still there. An expanse fills the space between them, but you have memory of each dot and where you placed the point of your pencil in the soft dirt of the yard. The dots exist, but they do not appear. Still, you have faith that they are there because there is evidence (if you will go back and check where you drew them).

7. Imagine the dots to be the body of Adam, expanded by the glory. Or they could represent the body of an angel or of the Lord Himself, present in your realm, but not seen with the naked eye. A week from now, you could walk right through the center of those four dots, representing the whole of one of those illustrations, and not even know it, because the whole silly thing will have slipped from your mind. If you sell your home and yard to someone else and do not tell them about the dots you drew there, that will not erase the dots. They will remain, but no one will perceive them. Just because you can't see them does not mean that they have ceased to exist.

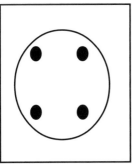

Illustration #1

When the glory of God was removed, Adam perceived that he had no mantle and was naked.

Illustration #1 shows the top, the bottom, the right and the left sides of a substance in a cohesive format that may be easily dominated and perceived.

In Illustration #2, we have expanded the time and distance between the molecules of the substance, and the result is that now it is no longer as easily perceived, and neither is it so dense.

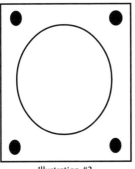

Illustration #2

As a third illustration, do you not now find it more difficult to perceive the dots on the four corners of the full illustration than in illustration #1?

I am convinced that this is how the dusty, scattered bodies of the dead are in the eye and mind of God. He purposefully put them together in their mothers' wombs by patterns formed before all of time. He recalls each boundary (like the four dots representing the top, bottom, left and right sides). One day, He will draw the scattered atoms and molecules and particles back together, and whole glorified bodies will stand before Him by the millions. Just as easily, He can do this for those who have faith to believe for re-creative miracles here today. God has the memory of every missing part.

> NOW faith is the substance of things hoped for, the evidence of things not seen.
> Hebrews 11:1

In the same manner, angels can be right next to you, and you may not know it. They are fully expanded beings of another realm. Great levels of light and glory travel between the molecules of their bodies. They are able to pass through an entire universe faster than the speed of light or sound. But when God tells them to appear to you, walking even as men, they obey.

> Man did eat the bread of angels; He sent them food in abundance.
> Psalm 78:25, NAS

> Be not forgetful to entertain strangers: for thereby some have entertained angels unawares.
> Hebrews 13:2

In my vision, I saw angels simply leave their bountiful blessing of glory behind. This caused them to appear as men. The substance of their celestial bodies was no longer expanded by invisible glory or scattered to an invisible level. Instead, it was condensed and solid and perceivable. Jesus left His glorious position in Heaven as the third person of the Trinity, to descend into the belly of a virgin and be conceived of the Holy Spirit, as a baby, to become a man. He then was filled with resurrection glory to return to the heavenly position forever. He was great in stature, but He left His glory behind to become small and earthly.

The universe is elastic, able to be expanded as it is flooded with God's *Oceans of Glory*. It may be disbanded or collapsed all together, or partially, as various levels of judgment fall upon it, should God choose to withdraw His glory. As great levels of glory and light are reduced, the molecules and atomic particles of angelic or celestial bodies become closer and closer together, leaving little distance between them. The density increases ... until they are easily perceived by the naked eye.

This would be like going back to the four corners of your yard and recovering the dots one by one and placing them back inside the circle of your ring in your palm where we started our illustration. As you walk around the yard collecting the dots you drew, lifting them up from the dirt or redrawing them one by one on your hand, the image of the whole would begin to reappear and be perceived, piece by piece.

This might remind you of the mysterious fragmented pictures in a children's coloring book, vague images of something waiting to be seen once you have converted the dots into lines. It might be very difficult to connect the dots in your imagination — if you didn't first know what they were to end up as. To find out what the picture was, you needed a tool, a crayon or a pencil.

We sense miracles and visions. Earthly and heavenly images and realities are all around us. The atmosphere is often pregnant and supercharged with expectancy in revival and prayer services, but we need a tool to access it, to connect it all from one realm to another. We need faith, filled up with glory.

We sense miracles and visions. Earthly and heavenly images and realities are all around us.

The Lord showed me how He walked through the walls of the Upper Room. I saw that the molecular structure of the limestone walls was of a certain density. Jesus left some of the glory of His resurrected body behind and condensed Himself into the density of the three-dimensional realm in which humans live. He approached the stone wall, and still contained some of the glory that kept the molecules in His body expanded. When He met the wall, He slipped through the molecules of the stone like a honeycomb and continued reducing the levels of glory until His flesh was tightly compacted and knit together as it had once been on earth. The disciples perceived Him, and Thomas examined His wounds.

We need faith, filled up with glory.

Drawn Up

When Jesus left the Upper Room that day, He drew upon the glory and filled back up with it again, expanding all the particles and molecules of His body, until the disciples could no longer see Him, much as the vapor from a tea kettle dissipates into the atmosphere of a room, the water turning into air. Jesus slid through the molecules in the door and was very large, now fully dominating the room that had just dominated Him. He was everywhere at once. The room and the city and the disciples were all inside of Him, as He continued to expand with the glory. He truly never left them or forsook them at all. They simply could not perceive Him, nor how very near He actually was and is, everywhere at once omnipotent, omnipresent.

Oral Roberts received a lot of flak from the news media and some pious Christians in the 1980s when He said that he, too, had seen Jesus as tall as a skyscraper. But Brother Roberts actually built the wonderful building he saw in his vision and put a medical center in it. How can we put God in a box? He is the great Creator of the universe and galaxies beyond.

After the Lord showed me these things in my 1980 experience, I said, "Okay, Lord. This is enough. This is about all I can handle." But He yearns to stretch us.

Jesus wasn't through with my audience yet, and I realized that I wasn't going anywhere until He was. My body was still caught up in worship down below in the civic center, and I didn't know my way out of that heavenly place either. So I continued to look on and see what He wanted to show me.

Jesus drew my attention back to the boy I had seen Him stand behind, when He had commanded me to receive creative miracles in my ministry. He said, "I know what that missing arm on this boy standing here used to look like." Hallelujah! Jesus then took the boy's arm and, in the twinkling of an eye, ran His hand down the arm and over each of the joints of each finger. Then the Lord cupped His fist, holding it up in front of me.

I asked, "What did You do?"

He said, "I took knowledge of it. I have a mold. On the day that your knowledge becomes full, so will your faith."

Then He clapped His hands and said, "Light be!" It was not an ordinary clap. It thundered and rippled through the universe and echoed on the inside of my body and made it tingle.

The Companion Bible [7] shows that when Jesus raised Lazarus from the dead, He "groaned like a war horse." His groan turned Hell and the grave upside down and inside out. Like the black hole of the nothingness of Genesis 1:2, God turned nothing into something, death into life, and altered the laws of physics again. Like a nuclear blast on a piece of uranium, light and glory burst forth into that tomb, and a dead man lived again and moved from the past to the future.

Recently, Ronnie and I were watching a video of A.A. Allen and saw that he quite often clapped just before a creative miracle took place. This really blessed me to see a confirmation of what I had seen in my heavenly visitation in 1980. As the Lord clapped, I stood there amazed at that sound and the burst of light.

Then Jesus said, "Glory, be!" and again there was a repeat of the same sequence of events.

Then He said, "Dust, be!" and released His hand. As He did, a small pile of glittering, light-filled "dust" appeared in His hand. It looked just like the "gold dust" we are now seeing, drawn out of Heaven seemingly from nowhere. Each time I have seen it since, it is usually when a creative miracle has taken place in my ministry or in the ministry of another.

Jesus had what looked to me to be about a half-dollar-sized portion of it in His hand, after He clapped and said, "Light be! Glory be! Dust be!" I've since learned, from reading a medical journal, that if you dehydrated all of the fluids out of a full-grown, six-foot eight-inch man's arm, you would be left with a pile of dust the size of a half dollar. Hmm ... I didn't know that back then.

Jesus took that dust, and He sprinkled it on the other side of the boy's body where there should have been a right arm, but there was none. Suddenly, where I had noticed nothing before, there was an image that caught my eye, as it followed the hand of Jesus sprinkling that dust. I saw a mold of an arm that should have been there, but was not. It was exactly like the one the Lord had measured "to take knowledge of it."

Jesus shouted, "Dust, be! Arm, be!" and, suddenly, the dust and the glory sound of Heaven married together, and there was an arm.

A few years ago, I happened to catch a broadcast on television that addressed the chronic syndrome known as "phantom limb." Patients who have undergone the amputation of a limb often complain that they can still feel that limb, like some phantom. Often, these cases are so serious that the patients must be referred to psychologists. I am convinced that the reason these people feel that their severed limbs are still there is that they *are* still there — in the spirit. The spirit has memory of every missing part, and so does Heaven. It is in the heart of God. He will use that information one day to restore each missing part to create a glorified whole.

If the entire body of that amputee was dead, then the spirit would be *"absent from the body"* and *"present with the Lord"* (2 Corinthians 5:8). But the arm or leg part of that human spirit can not go to be with the Lord. That bodily part is absent, and yet the spirit is still attached to the rest of the body. The part of that person's spirit belonging to that missing limb is hung in limbo between life and death, Heaven and earth, not able to be with the Lord, nor yet able to be glorified and whole. If that person is Hell-bound, not saved, then that part of him that is in limbo between two realms may already actually be experiencing torment by demon power. Or, even if the person is saved but not aware of how to fight by faith, the devil may be trying to torment him in this same way.

Medical science has never completely solved the great mystery of how to deal with the agony of these people. I feel great compassion for them, and so does Jesus.

I marveled at the restoration of the missing limb that Jesus performed in front of my unbelieving eyes. Wow! I had just received my first healing lesson. I was commissioned to accept and press in to a ministry of creative miracles. Now what?

Jesus said, "I'm putting you back to earth, but I'm taking you *here* first," and

He took me to a place of prayer. He said, "You'll not move out in any of this until you've prayed through."

Fellow members of the Body of Christ, you'll not move out like God wants you to until you become a worshiper, spending time, coveting your audience with God more than anything on the face of the earth. That means that relationships must change, and some will be discontinued, if you are to walk in the glory of God. And you will find that if you have lost your audience with God, you will lose your audiences with men.

 You'll not move out in any of this until you've prayed through.

I came back to the earthly realm out of that 1980 experience to a quiet auditorium. But later that night, in the evening service, there was a sudden burst of sound like the roar of a jet engine in the auditorium. Many testified about it, although no one in the morning service where I had been drawn out into the trance, had heard it then as I had. Many saw a wave curl over the auditorium that evening and testified of that, too, as great healings took place all across the congregation, as the minister walked down the aisles. It was a corporate event. We were drawn out into the glory. What will we do with it now?

ENDNOTES

1. Ice was a substance unknown in the desert climate of Egypt. Hail was the only sample they had ever seen. *Qapha*, OT:1087, Strong's, "a primitive root: to shrink, i.e. thicken (as uncorked wine, curdled milk, clouded sky, frozen water)."
2. Not to be confused with the religion of Christian Science, which we do not acknowledge nor approve.
3. According to scientific researchers, the highest known velocity in the physical universe is the velocity of light. Its current value was defined in 1967 at 299,792.4358 kilometers per second. Most scientists round that figure off to closely 3 X 108 meters per second, or 186,000 miles per second. (It is approximately one foot per nanosecond, or the distance light will travel in normal circumstances in one billionth of a second).
4. See the endnote in Chapter Six concerning the research of Norman and Setterfield on the theory of tired life.
5. Not only do I believe that this scripture obviously refers to the ordinance of Old Testament Law, but that it possibly has two facets. One of them may include the handwriting of DNA double helix, which science has recently nicknamed the "Book of Life" because of its effect on each cell and human form. There was wide media coverage of that subject in the fall of 2000. KJV calls the written code *"handwriting."*
6. Science states that light is the most constant force in the universe. Isn't it interesting that the Ancient of Days is seen as light and is the glory! Jesus is *"the light that lighteth ... the world"*! Einstein observed that material objects grow heavier as they are accelerated forward at the speed of light. Mass (m) of an object hurdled at velocity (v) will be heavier than the rest of the mass. These theories have been proven at the world-famous two-mile-long linear electron accelerator at Stamford University.
7. The Companion Bible, Kregal Publications (Grand Rapids, MI).

CHAPTER

ELEVEN

PRAYER, THE OCEAN PORTAL

Now there was a man of the Pharisees, named Nicodemus, a ruler of the Jews. This man came to Jesus by night and said to him, "Rabbi, we know that you are a teacher come from God; for no one can do these signs that you do, unless God is with him."

Jesus answered him, "Truly, truly, I say to you, unless one is born anew, he cannot see the kingdom of God."   John 3:1-3, RSV

The *Oceans of Glory* may best be previewed through the portals of prayer in the life of Jesus. If you track the signs and wonders ministry of Jesus carefully, you will note two things: Miracles occurred after He had been on the mountaintops of prayer, filling up, and after He had taught the Word. The Spirit of prayer and the anointing on the Word agree.

In the prayer garden, Nicodemus seemed to comprehend the subject matter of Jesus' prayer project. Quickly and briefly, he got to the point of his visit. Nicodemus either had been watching the signs and wonders ministry of Jesus or had heard about it. He said:

> *"Rabbi, we know that you are a teacher come from God; for no one can do THESE SIGNS THAT YOU DO, unless God is with him."*

Unlike Nicodemus, there are many people today who don't want anyone to make a fuss about signs and wonders. They want everything to be kept hush-hush. It is their feeling that the hysteria over a miracle represents a low, fleshly level of spirituality. Nothing could be further from the truth!

Jesus was a man of miracles, and He told a man who received a miracle to go show himself to the priests. [1] As a result, people all over Israel spoke of Jesus and His wondrous, heavenly touch.

Thousands of people drew attention to the Master's hand. The only ones who tried to hush up the news were the hypocrites and the Pharisees. Why did they do it? Perhaps it was because they were jealous that there was no such power in their camp.

Have you noticed that the world is not bursting into our churches to pray or to hear our theology on salvation? They are staying away by the droves. It is of no concern to them to hear about yesterday's revelations or miracles. They are not overly concerned about the Bible. Many of them have dusty versions of it on their coffee tables at home. What they want to know is whether our Jesus can heal their problems NOW.

There is a man-made saying that preachers sometimes repeat, quoting other preachers and not the Bible. It goes like this: "Seek God's face, not His hand." Those who repeat this cliche try to base their teaching on the prayer instructions of Jesus in Matthew's gospel, where Jesus said: *"Seek ye first the Kingdom of God ..., and all these things shall be added unto you"* (6:33). Yet, the historically accurate biblical account of Jesus clearly shows that the multitudes came to seek His hand. They came, hurting, bleeding, dying and desperate for a miracle touch of that famous hand. Still, although they all came to seek His hand and He knew it, He did not rebuke them. He did, however, caution them to take the greater joy in the fact that their names were written in Heaven (see Luke 10:20).

We are to seek God's face for fellowship and worship, but once having entered into the holy place of His presence, we are allowed to seek His hand, make our request, argue our case, put Him in remembrance of His promises and take home "the goods." In God's presence, what you need may well overtake you — whether you seek it or not. *"He is a rewarder of those who diligently seek Him"* (Hebrews 11:6, NKJ).

His Word declares:

> *Let us therefore come boldly unto the throne of grace, that we may obtain mercy, and find grace to help in time of need.*   Hebrews 4:16

Nicodemus came to Jesus in much the same way. He did not come seeking after the theology of eternal salvation on that night. This sacred doctrine was unknown to even the disciples prior to the death and resurrection of the Lord. Nicodemus came for one thing, a clue as to how to perform signs and wonders and miracles.

Nicodemus knew that not even Jesus could accomplish this unless God was with Him, and that could only happen in the experience of prayer, the act of drawing near to God's presence. That is why Nicodemus followed Jesus to the garden, boldly interrupting the hallowed event of prayer.

Prayer, the Ocean Portal

Nicodemus and the Born-Again Theme

Nicodemus had wanted to know how Jesus performed such signs and miracles, but the answer Jesus gave is hidden in a scripture that is so familiar to us that we may miss its simple meaning. Many Christians are well-acquainted with the third chapter of John's gospel because of the salvation passages in John 3:7 and 3:16:

Ye must be born again.

For God so loved the world that he gave his only begotten Son, that whosoever believeth in him should not perish, but have everlasting life.

Because of these well-known passages, the chapter is considered by many to be such a simple and basic portion of this gospel that it is often overlooked as a subject needing deeper study. Sometimes, however, the things that are most familiar to us actually hold the deeper and more complex solutions for life's most challenging questions.

For instance, consider the peanut. We eat roasted peanuts at the ballpark by the bagful. They are simple, small and ordinary. To George Washington Carver, however, the peanut was a miracle waiting to be discovered. In a book entitled *The Man Who Talks With Flowers,* [2] the story of his prayer life is told. He was a poor descendant of southern slaves, with no hope of escaping poverty. But he knew God, and he knew how to pray. A child, or even a slave, can open the portal of Heaven and cause *Oceans of Glory* to gush forth upon his or her life.

The Holy Spirit led George Washington Carver to hold the peanut (that grew in abundance in that region) in his hand and to ask it, "Tell me your secrets." Through this process, he discovered more than a hundred uses for the peanut. They included medicine, oil and cosmetics. Thus, George Washington Carver, descendant of slaves, received the potential to become a millionaire many times over through his discoveries.

John chapter three is a jewel like the simple peanut. It holds much more power within it than first meets the eye. Let us take a closer look at this familiar chapter and see what we may have missed.

First, we should note the scene, the characters and the plot. Jesus was praying in His prayer garden. He was a man of habit, He had a well-beaten path to the throne of God, and He probably used the same spot to pray whenever He was in Jerusalem, or Bethany, — Gethsemane. How else would Nicodemus, and later Judas, have known where to find Him?

Oceans of Glory

Jesus Christ is the same yesterday and today and forever.
Hebrews 13:8, NIV

Many people who need prayer in an emergency get into trouble because they have no knowledge of how to reach God at their moment of need. They have never forged a familiar path to His throne in prayer and cannot find the portal to enter in. So they either call an intercessor who does know how to get through or they perish in hopelessness. Later, of course, they want to blame God.

The pathway to miracles is through faith and a habitual, holy, Spirit-led life of prayer. Practicing the presence of God is praying *"without ceasing,"* as Paul wrote.

In answering Nicodemus' question about how to get the power for miracles, signs and wonders, Jesus directed His attention to the matter at hand in the prayer garden. He explained to the Pharisee that he must be born again from above, where there is a vast supply. ³ Only then could he see the Kingdom of God, the heavenly realm where miracles are stored up.

The connotation of the phrase *"Ye must be born again"* in the Hebrew mind, does not translate as "Get your fire insurance from Hell and make sure you barely slip into Heaven. Whew!" No. How shallow we have made this statement! And how light-mindedly the masses of Christians have lived the "born-again" life!

In both ancient and modern times, Jews have referred to both prayer and water baptisms as the experiences that can "renew." The mikva, or baptismal bath, is an integral part of Jewish practice, too. The idea of washing one's sins away in a consecrated body of water or bath was familiar to the crowds that John the Baptist addressed on the banks of the Jordan River. Thus, Jesus, as a Jew, also participated. When He did, the portals of Heaven opened that day, and God spoke: *"This is My beloved Son, in whom I am well pleased"* (Matthew 3:17, NKJ). Jesus spoke of both water and prayer in describing the "born-again" experience to Nicodemus.

The Middle Eastern mind would more correctly have understood this statement *"Ye must be born again"* as "Be changed from glory to glory! Daily be renewed and refreshed. Pass through the fire of God's presence until yesterday's dross is purified, and then *('the pure in heart shall see God')*, see the Kingdom! Come up hither!"

Yes, there is a once-in-a-lifetime commitment to Christ to be made and a sinner's prayer to be prayed, but this passage in John is far more than a starting point. It carries us to the finish line, beckoning every believer to come ever closer to the heart of God, pressing in today further than yesterday, pressing in more in this hour than in the last. It means: "Move on into a new and higher spiritual stance, breaking through Heaven's celestial wave, until the revelation power of those levels of prayer causes you to have open spiritual eyes to see the Kingdom glories." These are throne-room experiences, catchings-away to the place where miracle anointings will flow to and through you!

 Yes, there is a once-in-a-lifetime commitment to be made to Christ and a sinner's prayer to be prayed.

If you are not in a nearer and dearer and higher place in your prayer life with Jesus today than you were yesterday, you may be slightly backslidden already! That may hurt some, but think about it. Why coast on one experience, when God is an ocean, whose depths cannot be sounded and whose shores know no bounds?

I think that sometimes we do new converts a great disservice. We quote them half of this scripture, *"You must be born again,"* but we don't go on to say that then they will be able to *"see"* the Kingdom of God. Because of this, many run around all of their Christian lives as though blind. "Does any prophet have a word for me, please? I'm spiritually blind. I can't see or discern the will of God for my life." This can lead to the blind leading the blind. We should, instead, get new converts filled with the Spirit and encourage them to expect the supernatural in their prayer lives, to be like amphibious creatures, able to live in two realms at once, land and water, or earth and in heavenly places.

 God is an ocean, whose depths cannot be sounded and whose shores know no bounds.

Jesus was trying to let Nicodemus know that we can qualify for miracle ministry if our lives are holy and if we pray and press through daily and habitually, elevating our spiritual stance in God. We can never exhaust the depths of God.

> *Beloved, if our heart condemn us not, then have we confidence toward God. And whatsoever we ask, we receive of him, because we keep his commandments, and do those things that are pleasing in his sight.*
> 1 John 3:21-22

Once you are endowed with gifts to minister, you must be like the wind or the water that moves, not hemmed in by tradition that has no life. God must be allowed to control your life and your schedule, so that He can send you to the hungry people in due season, so that they can receive their miracles.

A miracle-signs-and-wonders people are not to be fleshly and carnal, but spiritual (touched by the waters of glorious baptisms). There is a signs-and-wonders "bunch" who have actually been in so much trouble because of their flesh that they have shipwrecked their ministries, and some have even slipped all the way to Hell.

To those who have never "cleaned up their acts" or matured in the fruits of the Spirit and intimate fellowship with Him, the Lord warns:

> "Not everyone who says, 'Lord, Lord,' will enter the kingdom of heaven, but only he who does the will of my Father who is in heaven. Many will say to me on that day, 'Lord, Lord, did we not prophesy in your name, and in your name drive out demons and perform many miracles?' Then I will tell them plainly, 'I never knew you. Away from me, you evildoers!' "   Matthew 7:21-23, NIV

Uh, oh! Whom is Jesus talking about? He is not speaking of the world, nor of the unsaved. No! How many psychics have you ever heard prophesy in the name of Jesus? They want credit for their divinations, so they never mention His name. This verse is referring to churched people who know the "Christianese" language and how to imitate or to participate for a season in the miraculous.

Judas participated in the miracles, the prayers and the fellowship with Jesus. He was a friend and companion of the most famous preacher who ever lived, and even that did not save him from the choices of his flesh. His end was eternal damnation, because he had no real connection with the throne room of Heaven.

Even if the most popular magazines and television stations report a "revival," the hollow thing will eventually shatter like an egg — if it is not born of holy prayer. It has happened before, and it will happen again.

How quickly the wind of blessing can become a gale of judgment for that which refuses to change! Jesus warned Nicodemus of this, letting him know of his weak spiritual condition. He informed Nicodemus that he did not understand earthly things, never mind the heavenly.

It was as if Jesus was saying, "Okay, Nicodemus, since you interrupted My prayer time, we will just turn this night into prayer school. Do you want to know how I get this power for miracles? I nightly press My spiritual position higher into the throne room, and I do it again and again. Then I flow like the wind and move like a river in the plans of God that I obtain. I am able to do this because, as we currently speak, I am seated with My Father in heavenly places — right NOW!"

> If I have told you earthly things, and ye believe not, how shall ye believe, if I tell you of heavenly things? And no man hath ascended up to heaven, but he that came down from heaven, even the Son of man which IS in heaven.
> John 3:12-13

Can't you just imagine Nicodemus blinking back at Jesus when He said that? "What do you mean, Jesus, by the words *'even the son of man which IS IN heaven'*?" I can see You, touch You, and You are nowhere but here. I see a three-dimensional You sitting here in this garden."

Jesus had not spoken of the past, as He was quoted elsewhere in the gospels as doing: *"As Abraham was, so am I."* He had not spoken of the future, as He did when He said, *"I will be resurrected in three days."* No, Jesus said that at that VERY moment, as they conversed, he was *currently* IN Heaven!

How was that possible? Jesus was being the *ekklesia*, "the caught-away ones," the forerunner of His own Church that would follow Him into the ministry of signs and wonders later on, as is recorded in the book of Acts.

From the foundations of the world, Jesus, the Lamb of God, had been slain. He always was, is and will be. A wheel within a wheel, He could watch eternity revolve around Himself in that garden of prayer. Caught up to a heavenly position, He had a bird's-eye view and was able to "see" the Kingdom. The "spirit of seeing and knowing" was upon Jesus in that place (see John 3:3).

Beyond the lower realms of men, who only hope and imagine, pray and confess, and tug and yearn with faith, Jesus was in the "NOW" place of Hebrews 11:1:

> *NOW faith is the substance of things hoped for, the evidence of things not seen.*　　　　　　　　　　　　　　　　　　　　　　Hebrews 11:1

Throne-Room Faith

(The realm of seeing and knowing, creative miracles and the gift of faith)

Overflowing Faith

Full Faith

Saving Faith

No Faith

Jesus was fellowshipping with the rest of the Trinity in the "gift-of-faith" level, throne-room faith, a place above ordinary faith, a spiritual position of creative miracles. In God's *Oceans of Glory*, the *Shamayim* of Heaven, where there are no limits, He could see the fullness of the Kingdom. It was easy for Him to reach up and grab the miracles of the raising of Lazarus, the opening of the blind eyes and the cleansing of the leper and tuck them into His bosom for the next day's tasks.

There are different levels of faith in this world. Some people have no faith. Then they hear the Gospel (*Faith cometh by hearing, and hearing by the Word of God*), and they receive saving faith. Then they get baptized in the Holy Spirit, and they have fullness of faith. Then they begin serving God and praying and hearing from the Holy Spirit, and some receive overflowing faith and can bless more than themselves. Then, there are those who pray through the veil of earth and have great communion with the Father, and they see visions of Heaven and hear His instructions for earth-changing ministry and come to throne-room faith. These receive orders from headquarters. They are a bold and confident, miracle-working group raised up from their prayer closets to do exploits in God.

Jesus had been discussing a timeline with Nicodemus in the beginning of this chapter that confounded the man, and this was the icing on the cake. What a mind-boggling concept! Nicodemus could not understand the idea of being suddenly cleansed, as if you had no past, or how you could return to your mother's womb. Now he was being hard-pressed to comprehend how one could sit with God in the future of Heaven, even as His body presently sat on a rock in a garden under a tree on earth talking to him in the flesh. [4] Eternity is a difficult concept for the carnal and finite mind of man, but in its realm and in a person's capacity to tap into it are the miracles and power that Nicodemus came searching for that night.

 "Rabbi, we know that you are a teacher come from God; for no one can do THESE SIGNS THAT YOU DO, unless God is with him."

On the timeline of eternity, Jesus left glory to take a dip into the wedge of thirty-three years of time, coming through the womb of a woman to live and to die on earth. But now He lives on in a resurrected body into eternity — forever. He is already up there looking into the wheel within a wheel, as time passes by, as one might imagine an ant sitting on the axle of a bicycle wheel watching the tire outside the spokes revolve around it.

Jesus is out there looking back on His life, on your life and even on the millennium, as though it were all past tense. If you are saved and living right, your heart condemning you not, and are assured of your salvation without a doubt, then guess what? If you make it to Heaven, you, too, will be in eternity looking back on the time in which we now live. In eternity, you will see the past and present and future all on the same page. That's exactly what Jesus was trying to help Nicodemus see that night.

> *And hath raised us up together, and made us sit together in heavenly places in Christ Jesus: that in the ages to come he might shew the exceeding riches of his grace in his kindness toward us through Christ Jesus.*
>
> Ephesians 2:6-7

Jesus was literally sitting in the flesh in the garden in His time, borrowing from Heaven all He could *"see"* in future time (from the resurrected, glorified bodies of Lazarus and others, their missing body parts), for the here and now. The greatest regret we may experience in Heaven will be the realization of all we could have possessed and brought to our time by prayer, but did not. God will have to wipe away our tears over our failed prayer lives and failed potential. Praise God that He has promised to do just that!

If we will pray in the Spirit, we will be able to access the bounty of Heaven for miracle power, even for the restoration of missing parts. Since God has memory of every missing part, then all of our glorified bodies are already in store for us there, awaiting the day of resurrection. Jesus is truly the Lord of time and space.

Nicodemus left the prayer garden that night realizing that he didn't know it all. He became a believer and follower of Jesus and assisted in the retrieval of the body of our Lord from the cross.

Let us search the *Oceans of Glory* sincerely, entering into depths of prayer, where we have never been before, and finding throne-room faith for the needs of our generation. Let us be a people approved of God by miracles, signs and wonders.

ENDNOTES

1. This was the proper thing to do in such a case, as dictated by the Law of Moses.
2. Glenn Clark, *The Man Who Talks With Flowers; the Intimate Life Story of Dr. George Washington Carver*, Macalester Park Publishing Co. (Saint Paul, MN: 1939)
3. NT:509 AGAIN: *anothen* (an'-o-then); from NT:507; "from above"; by analogy, "from the first"; by implication, "anew." (KJV, *from above*) again, "from the beginning (very first), the top." (Biblesoft's New Exhaustive Strong's Numbers and Concordance With Expanded Greek-Hebrew Dictionary, copyright © 1994, Biblesoft and International Bible Translators, Inc.)

4. Modern physics allows the mathematical invention of hypothetical particles which may or may not later be proved to exist. Thus, some have suggested that particles known as "tachyons" exist in the no-signal regions for normal human perception of past, present and future realms. Such particles would travel faster than the speed of light, approaching it only as a lower limit. If tachyons exist, they would (theoretically) provide a mechanism for communication faster than the speed of light (Divine thought).

It is significant to note that if the velocity of light had been higher in the past, as I believe it was, then the size of the "no-signal zones" would have been smaller in the ages past. This would have allowed more physically observable information into our world of experience than is now accessible. I am speaking of physical and observable, not spiritual information.

Adam, in his unfallen state, may have been able to see into the glory realm more frequently and more easily than we can.

CHAPTER

TWELVE

THE CARRIED-AWAY ONES

After that, we who are still alive and are left will be caught up together
with them in the clouds to meet the Lord in the air. And so we will be with the
Lord forever. Therefore encourage each other with these words.

1 Thessalonians 4:17-18, NIV

Many impossible journeys of faith will be accomplished in the days ahead with supernatural grace and provision. On every hand, believers will be testifying of trances and translations as our prayer lives intensify. Entire congregations may disappear and reappear in another location. Who knows? It is time to take the limits off of God. We might as well, for He will have His way — regardless of what we do.

Why should these things be difficult to believe? Ultimately, a significant portion of the population of the world will be translated in one massive miracle, the Rapture of the Church. The translations we experience now are a foretaste of this culminating event. Men and women of the Bible, such as Paul and John, were caught up in the Spirit and had unusual experiences, and evangelists through the centuries have had similar things happen to them. Some have received letters thanking them for the crusades they preached in other lands, when they knew very well they had never been there. For example, I have often heard the story told of Oral Roberts waking up with sand in his pants cuffs and having no knowledge whatsoever of how it got there. Shortly afterward, as the story goes, a thank-you card was to have arrived, acknowledging his crusade in a foreign land. He had no recollection of preaching that crusade. Caught in God's *Oceans of Glory*, we may travel far, from one shore to the other, in the deep of sleep.

The Greek word *ekklesia*, translated *church*, means the "carried-away or drawn-out ones" or "those belonging to the Lord." We are surely His, and He surely wants to carry us away in His glory:

> *Therefore, whether you eat or drink, or whatever you do, do all to the glory of God.*   1 Corinthians 10:31, NKJ

"Lost in God" would be an accurate way of describing the visions, dreams, trances and translations of many saints through the centuries. They entered a place in the realm of the Spirit where all earthly worries are temporarily suspended, and the obstacles to and the impossible distance involved in reaching the harvest of souls are removed.

 "Lost in God" would be an accurate way of describing the visions, dreams, trances and translations of many saints through the centuries.

How does God Almighty accomplish such things? This is nothing for Him. He is Lord of time and space. He is still sovereign and able to manipulate the molecular structure of angelic and human beings who yield to Him for His purposes — at the direction of the Spirit. Man dreams of such ways to travel because he was created for it before the Fall.

"Beam me up, Scotty!" was a phrase that delighted the "trekkies" who savored the hit television series "Star Trek." Although I was not one of those fans, I did catch a broadcast now and then and recall the scene that was idealized in that phrase. By way of laser and digital light beams, the cells of someone's body were translated. Then they were regathered into a whole being again in some other location.

Science-fiction script writers certainly have nothing new on God. He has been performing this act for thousands of years without the need for human science or man-made machines. And He has all the bugs worked out of His translation process. Nothing ever goes wrong.

Some people are resistant to such things, fearful of being embroiled unwittingly in the occult, or just fearful of any supernatural experience at all. People like that intensely fear the most supernatural experience of a lifetime, the one they cannot avoid — departure from this life either through death or through the Rapture.

Rev. Kenneth E. Hagin frequently tells a story to his audiences (and it has been taped often) about a woman in a wheelchair who was prayed for. God sent the power she needed to rise up and walk, but when she perceived the tangible force all around her, she resisted, from fear and disbelief, and clung tenaciously to her wheelchair. The change that was about to take place in her life was too much for her. God, not willing to allow the faith of the congregation to be confused or denied, proceeded to show His power by lifting her bodily from the chair. Still, she would not let go. What stubborn people we are sometimes! Is raising someone from a wheelchair difficult for a God who raises the dead?

Recently, at a dinner I attended, Mama Mary Jenkins, an evangelist who traveled with the famous Smith Wigglesworth and who has lived into her nineties to continue vigorous ministry, told a group of us (Ronnie and myself, Flo Ellers, Sandy Robbins, Ruby Caudill, Karen Loomis and Sheila Scott) an account of Smith Wigglesworth raising a dead child from his coffin. The boy had been dead for several days. When Smith spied the funeral procession, God's power, mercy and grace came upon him, and the child was raised. This so affected the boy's father that he ran screaming from the scene and was not found until three days later.

They eventually found him in a livery stable. The same glory that had raised his dead son had healed him of a limp that had afflicted him for years, but he was delirious with a high fever. Some people are terrified of the very things their hearts most intensely desire. Certainly this man desired to receive his son again, but the flood of glory that accomplished the act was more than he had bargained for.

My husband, Ronnie, often says, "We are living today in the position of life with which we are currently satisfied." If this were not so, men and women would press harder, faster, longer and deeper in to the presence of God. They want to blame Him for their ills and accuse Him of not caring to mend them, but if He were to answer, it would be with much more glory and responsibility than some of them are willing to accept.

Ronnie and I have often prayed for people who needed healing in multiple areas of their bodies. One man wanted to get rid of his allergies, but when Ronnie volunteered to pray for the healing of his legs and back, he was quick to remove from him. "No! Oh, no! Don't you dare do that!" he protested. "I would lose my disability check, and then what would we do?"

What a foolish attitude to take! Could not the same God who heals such impossible maladies lead this man into a new job or some other financial miracle?

Most of those who have received supernatural experiences along this line do not meet many with whom they can find common ground. But this is changing. In the coming *Oceans of Glory*, many will corporately experience these things, even as they did in the days of the Bible:

> *After that, he appeared to more than five hundred of the brothers at the same time, most of whom are still living, though some have fallen asleep.*
>
> 1 Corinthians 15:6, NIV

Then a loud voice will shout from heaven, "Come up!" And they will rise to heaven in a cloud as their enemies watch.   Revelation 11:12, TLB

It was not long afterwards that he rose into the sky and disappeared into a cloud, leaving them staring after him. As they were straining their eyes for another glimpse, suddenly two white-robed men were standing there among them, and said, "Men of Galilee, why are you standing here staring at the sky? Jesus has gone away to heaven, and some day, just as he went, he will return!"   Acts 1:9-11, TLB

We were recently having lunch with Sister Billye Brim and members of her family and staff in Branson, Missouri. She told us of a meeting in January 2000 in Ozark, Alabama, where the following word of prophecy was given: "One reason the old-timers had more supernatural experiences, such as translations, was that they had greater respect for praying in tongues."

At that lunch, Shelli Brim Oaks told us of being translated one night. She observed people talking, and she prayed for them in a certain room, although they could not see her. Later, at a large campmeeting, she was introduced to these same people, and they had never met her. She didn't feel a release to tell them of her experience, but they kept staring at her. After a while, they said, "We feel we have met you before, but we can't place it."

When the End-Time Handmaidens of Ohio invited us to speak for them, we met an elderly saint. In spite of her great age and discomforts, she bravely attended the meetings, and we could not forget her sparkling blue eyes. The depths of love shone forth through them.

Years later, we returned to the same area for a Christmas concert, and my friend Geneva Chevernic brought this elderly lady to the concert. She let us know that the lady had been telling everyone, with a resolute affirmation, that I had visited her hospital bed the week before and, through prayer, raised her up from a death grip. Everyone knew that I had not been there at all. I had been in Oklahoma practicing for my Christmas concerts.

"But wait a minute!" I said, as the woman thanked me and I noticed that everyone smiled. "Maybe there is something to this. Last week I did have a very strange experience. While laboring late at night in my office on a newsletter, I suddenly had the sensation of lifting out of my body about five feet off the floor. If I could have grabbed the floor, I would have. I shook myself and wondered why such a strange feeling had gripped me.

The hour is too late! I was thinking. *I'd better get to bed!* I shrugged off the experience. After all, I hadn't been doing anything very spiritual at that moment. I was just singing or humming as I worked, practicing the presence of God as I learned to do long ago — but nothing else.

Sleep came quickly and uneventfully that night. Through a long day, I had more than earned it.

But, could it be true what this lady was saying? It was at night and the same week that she claimed I had come to her bedside and prayed for her. She revived the next day, and she had not been expected to live. Hmm ...

On another occasion, in the mid 1990s, I was preaching in California. I had never been to that state for preaching before, but the couple who picked me up at the airport insisted at their lovely diner that I had ministered in their old church during the 1980s. As the menus were removed and the waitress served tea, they said, "You brought your harp and your large mural of *The Travail of the Flag,* and you preached on the blood covenant."

That unique combination sounded very much like me. I was curious now. "And how long did I stay?" I prodded.

"Three nights," they said, without hesitation. "Are you going there again on this trip?" they asked. "Are you going to get in touch with the pastor?"

I did my best to explain that I did not know their pastor because I had never been to California before. No matter how coincidental it was that another minister had showed up with my "stuff" in imitation of me, it could not have been me. I could sense that I was spoiling the spirit of the dinner. As graciously as possible, I eased out of that subject and took the conversation in a smoother direction. But many questions were left unanswered. Hmm ...

Was I to believe that God not only translates people, but that He translates harps and paintings too? Why not? He came for Elijah in a chariot. He will one day cause an entire city (foursquare) to hover over Jerusalem:

> And I saw the holy city, new Jerusalem, coming down out of heaven from
> God, prepared as a bride adorned for her husband.   Revelation 21:2, RSV

Before the work began on my painting *The Travail of the Flag,* I had a most unusual experience. My job with two of NASA's semiretired space scientists in a private communications firm had ended. The space shuttle Challenger had blown up, and this forced them to return to NASA, as their expertise was required to get the project back on track. Though working with them had been enjoyable (and offers to stay on as a bis sister caretaker for their children were almost irresistible), I had to decline because of an urgent tug on my spirit to depart for full-time ministry. I had been invited to attend a missions conference in St. Louis, Missouri, with Sister Gwen Shaw. Had the job not ended, I would never have been able to participate.

The drive from Houston, Texas, to St. Louis in my little gold Volkswagen Beetle was much more than I desired to take on by myself. However, since no one was free to accompany me, and the promptings of the Spirit not to miss the conference were so great, I was compelled to go alone.

I had to leave without my final paycheck, which would arrive later in the summer, and I only had $14.00 cash in my possession. Credit cards would come later in life. When I was younger, I didn't yet have one.

As I began my journey, I filled up the gasoline tank, not just knowing how the Lord would provide for the balance of the trip. I knew many people in Tulsa, and several ministers there had invited me to stop and minister anytime I was going through, so I wasn't worried. I learned long ago that in order to cross uncharted waters, you have to begin, and God will do the rest.

How do you walk on water? One step at a time. When the Master extends His hand and His grace, you take hold of it and begin to take the first step. The important thing is never to look down. Peter taught us all how to navigate the seas quite well. A study of his life would be a very wise investment of time for all those who believe that *Oceans of Glory* are coming.

Casting my faith and my bread on the water once again, I was headed to St. Louis in that little gold car alone. I was singing in the Spirit, a wonderful aria, to no one's ears but God's and the angels'. What happened next was inexplicable to me. On $14.00 worth of gas, and in less than five hours, I had arrived in Tulsa. The next day I left with a cheery wave from the friends who had hosted me for the night and returned to my car. I had no money. So sweet had been our reunion and fellowship that I had completely forgotten the need for some sort of financial miracle, and it did not occur to me again until I had arrived in St. Louis, some five hours later.

Normally, it would have taken several hundred dollars to go that distance and about three times that many hours of driving time. God had translated me and the car, or He had sped up the driving time without causing me to break the road rules. Why? I wasn't sure.

Upon entering the Marriott Hotel lobby, I was greeted by a friend, Anita Christopher, who had felt led of the Lord to prepare a room for me. She had the room, meals and conference fee all paid for, with no true confirmation on my part that I was coming. She had stayed in the lobby all day as hundreds of attendees arrived, praying for me and waiting for my arrival. God had drawn us together over the miles and circumstances through prayer on both ends.

That's how translation works. It's like a telephone connection. You need a party on each end — someone calling out to God for assistance and someone else answering, "Send me, Lord, anywhere, anytime You need me. Here am I; send me." The Holy Ghost is the operator, and He makes the switchboard connection. Even the filmmakers of the past century sensed that the heavens were made for men to traverse — as well as the land and the seas. "Beam me up, Scotty!"

The generation that will go up in the Rapture will be quickened and prepared for such an experience. Fear-bound earthlings don't want to fly, but well-trained astronauts love it. Translations, visions, trances, dreams and the like will be key manifestations of the *Oceans of Glory* revival that is coming upon us. Can we believe for it?

Jesus will return for a people of faith, whose earthly mission is done and whose carnal weights have been cast off:

> *Wherefore seeing we also are compassed about with so great a cloud of witnesses, let us lay aside every weight, and the sin which doth so easily beset us, and let us run with patience the race that is set before us, looking unto Jesus the author and finisher of our faith.* Hebrews 12:1-2

The faith of God's people will cause them to go airborne.

Not only does the glory translate us to those in need, but the glory can also supernaturally draw them to us — willing, or even unwillingly. One night in Ontario, Canada, I had such an experience.

We had spent all week there preaching and taping a new series on God's divine order. On the last day, I intended to wear a white suit that night, but I found it spoiled with a spot which took me all afternoon to remove. While rubbing it out, I found that my prayer language kept welling up within me with a greater intensity than my current concern for the final sermon that evening. I followed the stream of prayer until the spot came out.

Later, I stood at my pulpit, very proud of having conquered the spot. I was wearing a clean white suite, and I was excited about completing the sermon "The God of Divine Order." It was not to be so.

Not far into my message, when I had reached the part about the kosher feast — the Seder, the feast of order, or feast of blood covenant — things suddenly went awry. Instead of sharing the illustration I had planned on one certain point, I was led to share something else and began telling the audience about an incident that happened in 1976 when a woman had been slain in the Spirit. She was very obese and became wedged in between the pew and the kneeling bench. This alarmed her ultrathin husband. Two local Episcopal priests were officiating the Charismatic service, and they began to discuss this situation. The problem was that they forgot to turn off their microphones first.

One said, "How do we get her out of this situation?"

The other replied with simple wisdom, "I don't know, but if the Holy Ghost got her into this mess, let Him get her out!" And, sure enough, in the fullness of God's time, the woman suddenly slipped out of the tight squeeze as easily as she had slipped into it. It reminded me of the way a greased pig slips through the hands of eager children at the county fair.

As I finished this illustration, my audience roared with laughter, and I was horrified. This did not follow my carefully laid plan and was destroying the perfect tape series I was recording. Quickly, I jerked myself back to the sermon and tried to find some way to bridge from the story I had just told back to the point I was making on things being kosher, orderly. But it was useless. Instead, all I could do was say, "Oh, well, pigs aren't kosher, are they?"

Again my audience roared, and I was quite at a loss for direction. A Dutch missionary of a stern countenance suddenly stood up and approached me at the pulpit. I thought, *Oh, boy! Now I'm in trouble. These Canadians are very conservative, especially the Dutch.*

The man said, "Sister Shelli, don't quench the Holy Ghost. The people need this refreshing!" I was amazed, for I had mistakenly braced myself to be rebuked. In response to him, I reached out one finger and lightly tapped his forehead, not following any protocol for such a situation, but feeling somehow that it was the right thing to do.

From that feather touch, he jerked backward and landed hard on the floor on his back. His legs began wildly bicycling in the air and continued for the next twenty minutes. (His missionary wife was sitting nearby in shock at what was happening. Later, I was told, she realized that she had received a miracle healing from cancer.) The audience roared with laughter at the humorous sight.

Again, I tried to bring things back into my understanding of church order, but when I reached for my sermon notes, the makeshift pulpit (a music stand) slid to the floor, and the notes were scattered. As I bent over to pick them up, I too was suddenly stuck, and I bent over with laughter. The corners of my mouth felt immobilized, as if I was drunk. Moments later, I was rolling on the floor in that perfectly white suit, not even knowing how I had gotten there, and most of the people were doing the same thing.

The pastor came to remove the pulpit, and he picked up the notes. He laughed too as he read out loud the bold, large-type letters I had laid out, "God Is a God of Divine Order!" Yes, He is, but not when we try to box Him in.

At the end of that evening, I saw one last little lady rolling next to me. She was the very one who had exhibited the most disgusted and frightened looks when the whole event had first started. I knew that if she could have found an exit at that first moment, she would have. An entire row of people had been hemming her in. Now, at the end of the evening, there she was, like a drunk, on the floor next to me. She was rolling and giggling and did not know either how she got there. God healed that lady that night of serious high blood pressure. Her doctor later confirmed it.

I am so glad God changed the order of that service, and I am glad that He got that spot of religious rigidness out of me, like the spot on my white suit.

As we left that place, the pastor told us of the Toronto Blessing, which was occurring about a hundred miles away. There this same manifestation of laughter and strange acts of God were also occurring. The glory waves had traveled in a hundred-mile radius to reach me that night, as I stood unawares in my pulpit. That experience changed my entire life and ministry forever.

This is nothing new. I have heard of the stories from St. Louis, Missouri, near the turn of the twentieth century, where Maria Woodworth-Etter held a tent meeting. It was poorly attended at first, but later, because of strange acts of the Holy Ghost, the tent became full. Mrs. Woodworth-Etter was caught away to Heaven in a trance of glory. She remained frozen in the Spirit with her hand uplifted for three days, void of all bodily functions except breath and heartbeat. She was in the epicenter of a glorious happening.

Within a hundred-mile radius of the tent, a strange phenomenon occurred, as though one should throw a stone and watch the ripples spread out across the surface of a pond. Unsuspecting people, working on their farms, began to faint and experience trances. Someone who knew about the tent meetings rounded up as many of the curiously stricken people as possible into the backs of wagons and drove them to the tent.

I heard about one agnostic woman who mocked the revival. While she was pumping water at her fancy little kitchen sink, she was suddenly overcome by the glory and fell into a trancelike state that caused her husband to think that she had had a stroke. This prideful woman's hand was frozen to the pump like a corpse. After the pump handle was removed with a wrench, they carried her to the tent in that condition, still attached to the pump.

When the tent was quite full, the Lord released Mrs. Woodworth-Etter from her trance, and she continued to preach the sermon which had been interrupted when she fell into the trance. The tent was now full of people eager to hear it. What a great method of advertising! Signs and wonders and miracles are better than newspaper ads.

Allow God to draw you out into the deep. Be patient and follow His Holy Spirit into the depths of glory, *"line upon line, precept upon precept."* Become a well of blessing, and let Him dig out a deep reservoir in you that will never disappoint a person in need.

Praise Jesus daily, commune with the Father in His Word and pray in the Spirit with the Holy Ghost, and you will be able to take the limits off of God and be one of the carried-away ones, in the *ekklesia*, the Church, the holy Bride!

THE RIPTIDE

What is the FIRE unless it is consuming?
What is the RAIN unless it is falling?
What is the WIND unless it is blowing?
What is the RIVER unless it is flowing into an OCEAN? [1]
— Shelli Jones Baker

As *Oceans of Glory* sweep over us in the days ahead, lives will be permanently changed. We will go from having a taste for the ordinary to walking, talking, eating, sleeping, praying, fasting and working in the glory. But even if you have learned to swim in the river, watch out for the ocean; it has a riptide.

The peaceful ebbs and flows of ocean waves rolling upon the shore and shimmering in the sunlight are only a surface illusion. Turbulent forces lie below the surface of the water. Church history, with its life-and-death battles for the souls of men, records both those who were victorious and those who failed. It tells of Olympic-style marathoners, who navigated and trained for the depths, and also of fools, who plunged in unprepared and drowned. This is evident in the first outpouring of the glory on the Church in the book of Acts. The first group touched by the Holy Ghost on the Day of Pentecost got into the river, and then those on the banks jumped into the act. Three thousand people rejoiced in the revelation of their salvation that day, wading and swimming into a new pool of refreshing, as God poured His glory out on *"all flesh."*

However, as the rivers turned into saturated *Oceans of Glory*, and prayer meetings and gatherings began to shake the city of Jerusalem and go all night long, the depths of glory hastened upon some unsuspecting ones. They had no respect for the Holy Spirit and His miracle power and had not learned to swim before they plunged, so they drowned. Touch the *Oceans of Glory* with responsibility, or do not touch them at all. But if you touch them, do so with all your might!

> *"I know your deeds, that you are neither cold nor hot. I wish you were either one or the other! So, because you are lukewarm — neither hot nor cold — I am about to spit you out of my mouth."*   Revelation 3:15-17, NIV

We should beware of the temptation to imitate the past instead of flowing with the current unique reality of each new day's visitation. God's mercy is daily renewed. Ananias and Sapphira seemed to be latecomers to the scene in Acts chapter 4. When they showed up late, they failed to understand the purity of the moment (see Acts 5:1-11).

It is not certain that Ananias and Sapphira were original members of the prayer group that was touched by the fervor and unction to sell all their goods and lay the proceeds at the apostles' feet. They may have just heard about the great idea, decided that it was a good thing and tried to "get on the bandwagon" of the spontaneous giving. They were out of line and didn't seem to have either the anointing or the calling to do what others were doing.

The copycat idea that came to Ananias and Sapphira cost them their lives, because their hearts were not right. They had not prayed through and gotten the strategy and direction of the Holy Ghost. When their muddled-up plans fell through, they lied to the Holy Ghost in Peter's ministry, and as a result, they were struck dead. Just like Adam and Eve, the first man and woman, Ananias and Sapphira sinned when they touched forbidden goods. God wanted their all.

 Touch the *Oceans of Glory* with responsibility, or do not touch them at all! But if you do touch them, do so with all your might!

You can't copy the last wave because the ocean is always moving. The important thing for all of us is to get our instructions — about money, location, sermon, methods of evangelism, music — everything — in the secret place of prayer.

The anthems of Azusa Street and Wales, Cane Ridge and the 1950s tent revivals will not necessarily be the sound needed for your city. While it is lovely to be able to purchase a CD recorded at one of the wonderful revival meetings of our time, listening to what was "hot" in one place is not the same as going before the throne of God for yourself and pulling down a unique sound for your city. That unique sound is there waiting in the *Oceans of Glory* to be drawn out when a psalmist in your ministry or church staff pays the price on his or her knees to find it. And when that happens, the people of your city will be following that one to the altars like the children followed the Pied Piper.

There's more, and I want to hear it. Don't you? "More, Lord, more!" Cry for it, and a trumpet will sound.

Everywhere I go, I challenge musicians to write ocean songs. We have enjoyed many good songs about the river, but it has come and gone. What about the oceans? There's more. "More, Lord, more!"

Worldly Pied Pipers have taken their cities with anthems — "New York, New York," "I Left My Heart In San Francisco," "By the Time I Get to Phoenix, She'll Be Gone," and "Chattanooga Choo Choo," to mention a few. I believe that Heaven has a certain sound, a trumpet to be heard, an anthem of revival for every church, city, state and region.

 I believe that Heaven has a certain sound, a trumpet to be heard, an anthem of revival for every church, city, state and region.

Many have brought reproach to the revival of the past few years. They journeyed in hunger to new wells of artesian purity for another drink as revival sprang up. But they errantly thought that they could force open the floodgates of revival in their home churches — with or without the harmonious agreement of the pastors. Disdain settled heavily upon the movement as new "Holy Ghost drunks" laughed through sermons when the Spirit wasn't calling for laughter anymore. Overriding the pleas of astounded pastors and irritated congregations, some people insisted in laughing on ... until churches were split because of it. Those who were affected by these tragedies had no chance to truly experience the original source of the well. Who wants to fly around the globe to a revival, when you feel that what came from that place is polluted?

In another sense of the word, such water cannot be carried far anyway. It would be akin to bringing fresh spring water home from the Swiss Alps to a dying friend on the other side of the globe. It's a great idea, but by the time you get the water home, it won't be fresh anymore. If you delay long, that once-fresh water could actually be growing bacteria and algae. For a truly pure drink, you have to get to the well yourself or dig through and open one in your own backyard. The river is here, was here, and is gone ... but what about the oceans?

Wise King Solomon declared:

> There is a time for everything,
> and a season for every activity under heaven: ...
> a time to weep and a time to laugh,

a time to mourn and a time to dance,
a time to embrace and a time to refrain,
a time to be silent and a time to speak.   Ecclesiastes 3:1-7, NIV

 The river is here, was here, and is gone ... but what about the oceans?

Experienced swimmers tackle marathons, while sunbathers need to be cautious in the shallows. Recently, we saw an e-mail in which someone was "throwing stones" again at fivefold ministry gifts, with the ancient, but tired argument that God does not need superstars anymore. Fortunately, the gifts that Jesus gave to the Church (see Ephesians 4) are just that, and He is not through with them — anymore than He is with the rest of the Bible. The article said: "Now God will use the nameless, faceless ones ... ."

Precisely because God loves people like these, He will not give them such a wide-open door at first. They wouldn't know what to do with it, and they would fall hard. They have not yet realized that the ministry seen on public platforms is only the tip of the iceberg. It may appear glamorous and a position to be coveted, but any long-haul-marathoner, pastor, evangelist or teacher, can tell you that the ministry is hard work. The arrival of *Oceans of Glory* will not change that. The work of the ministry will only increase in the days ahead.

During the Welsh Revival, seventy workers a day were needed around the altars for ministry. God always pours His glory out on platforms of excellence. They can bear the weight of it. A skyscraper in Japan crashed a few years ago because the contractors had used cheap bricks, containing too much sand. The glory will not fall hard on ill-prepared platforms.

In all my years of ministry, I have never seen God give a lazy man a ministry. Lazy people may be called and gifted with anointings, but because they are not diligent, they usually pass from the scene rather quickly. They often succumb to drowning. The successful revivalists of yesterday deserve much honor, and those of tomorrow will need intercessory prayer so that they can carry the torch consistently high for their generation.

It may appear that many new, no-name persons have suddenly arrived on the scene of Church history, but if you could interview them (as I have a few), you would quickly see that a common thread runs through their stories:

> *Jesus appeared to me when I was young. I trained a lifetime for this. I was mentored by a father [or mother] of previous revivals. I practiced my musical instrument hours a day. I prayed. I fasted and worked in their prayer lines.*

No one knew these people during their wilderness days, as they prepared to carry the torch. Saul knew nothing of David — when the lad was still busy practicing his harp and tending his sheep. But God shines a light on our long, hard nights and reserves His spotlights for those whose witness is bright because they have passed through the fire.

 But God shines a light on our long, hard nights and reserves His spotlights for those whose witness is bright because they have passed through the fire.

I have experienced the riptide myself. Since a breakthrough year of 1994, it seems we and other ministers we fellowship with have climbed higher and higher in heavenly anointings each time we have mounted a platform and stood behind a pulpit, and the surges of glory have only escalated. As I have said, in 1996, a supernatural fire hit my hands. It was so hot that it burst the band on my wedding ring and rearranged the prongs on the diamond. This didn't happen just once. It has happened over and over again, as I have prayed for creative miracles. People began walking away from wheelchairs, blind eyes started opening and many people received new knee joints.

Under that kind of anointing, it has, at times, proven difficult to walk off of a platform into the mundane atmosphere of daily life. This type of ministry requires going higher than most people care to function, to grab miracles for the people while the gates of Heaven are open in times of tangible anointing. Immediately upon leaving that atmosphere, you can feel the suction of the undertow grabbing fiercely at you. Every demon in the city seems to remember your name.

This is why we need well-trained and experienced men and women of prayer at work in prayer rooms behind the scenes. Not only should they be there in full force to intercede for the people and to believe God for their deliverance, but they should also be there to protect the people who minister in the meetings.

In one of A.A. Allen's videos, he spoke of a woman who was healed and delivered of a deaf spirit. The spirit jumped off of her and onto a woman standing next to her in the prayer line. This woman had not had any problem with her ears before, but she was now suddenly deaf. Evangelist Allen had to deal with that spirit a second time before the second woman could be healed.

When I sought the Lord, with a sense of responsibility for what happens in my prayer line, He let me know that it is impossible to keep touching such intense power without insulators. We need the "pray-ers," who should be on their knees throughout the duration of our events.

If the anointing is high in a service, we can sail in on the existing wave and then be able to take the meeting up even higher. We can sometimes reach a level of the glory that astounds us before we even know we've gotten there. Before and after meetings like that, it is necessary for us to get away to a solitary place, to spend time with Jesus and to thank Him. During such events, we need those who will stand watch in prayer.

Waves of revival glory are sweeping in upon us. Come gladly to the waters, but beware of the riptides. Pray.

ENDNOTE

1. Inspired, in part, by a sermon of Reinhard Bonke.

CHAPTER

FOURTEEN

WHO CAN RECEIVE THE OCEANS?

Oh how great is thy goodness, which thou hast laid up for them that fear thee; which thou hast wrought for them that trust in thee before the sons of men! Thou shalt hide them in the secret of thy presence from the pride of man: thou shalt keep them secretly in a pavilion from the strife of tongues.

Psalm 31:19-20

God's *Oceans of Glory* will not come upon just one branch of the Christian tree. They will flood us all.

I urge my Evangelical, Pentecostal, Charismatic and Catholic brothers and sisters to openly consider what God is doing among other parts of our very large and diverse family. He is drawing all the parts of His Body closer together in the end of this Church Age.

Why is it that so many fine Christians seem to claim that every miracle recorded by those of the other parts of our faith are automatically of familiar spirits or demonic origin? We must be careful not to judge so quickly, but to ask Jesus about this matter and heed His Word. For instance, there have been many hundreds of books written about the hatred between the Protestant and Catholic churches throughout the past thousand years. Such hatred surely saddens the heart of God. It is of Satan, and he thrives upon it. God is not the author of such things.

There have been plenty of "cranks" and many excesses on both sides of the aisle, and politicians in both camps have used existing differences to further their causes. But there have also been multitudes of earnest praying saints in both movements who have experienced the depths of God and His miracles.

Across the wide divide between Protestantism and Catholicism, an ocean must begin to flow. A tsunami is needed to flood the strongholds so that Holy

Ghost reconstruction may begin. I personally have seen the Lord at work recently in both camps

 Across the wide divide between Protestantism and Catholicism, an ocean must begin to flow.

Jesus' desire was that we all might be one:

> *And other sheep I have, which are not of this fold: them also I must bring, and they shall hear my voice; and there shall be one fold, and one shepherd.*   John 10:16

> *And now I am no more in the world, but these are in the world, and I come to thee. Holy Father, keep through thine own name those whom thou hast given me, that they may be one, as we are.*   John 17:11

> *That they all may be one; as thou, Father, art in me, and I in thee, that they also may be one in us: that the world may believe that thou hast sent me. And the glory which thou gavest me I have given them; that they may be one, even as we are one: I in them, and thou in me, that they may be made perfect in one; and that the world may know that thou hast sent me, and hast loved them, as thou hast loved me.*   John 17:21-23

How delighted I was some years ago to be invited by a priest in my hometown to preach in his church. He invited all the churches of the area and advertised it as ALL SOULS CRUSADE. We had a good turnout, and people were saved in the meeting. Years before that happened, a previous priest had let me use the same room to have a private prayer and praise time each morning. I would start singing from an Episcopal hymnal I carried, then progress to another hymnal, the *Pentecostal Melodies of Praise*, and then move to some folk-mass songs and Charismatic choruses. Eventually, the heavens would break open, and a lyrical melody of singing in tongues would burst forth from my spirit. I would stay there for hours, until it seemed that Heaven clothed me, and the room filled with God's presence.

On my last morning there, I received a word from the Lord about an upcoming trip to Italy. A brother from Campus Crusade for Christ had invited me and a roommate to stay with his family for the summer. The Lord let me know that when I got there, I should "sing the walls down." It was an assignment that I did not fully understand.

I was so carried away in rapturous praise, alone in that Catholic church, that

I never heard the cleaning lady come in ... until she dropped the broom. The clatter jarred me back to the reality of earth. She scampered out of the choir loft with apologies, but before she did, she asked, "Where did you learn to sing such beautiful arias in Latin? They are some of my favorites! Father has been listening every morning behind the door over there too!"

I did not know Latin. The miracle of this was only a foretaste of something greater on my upcoming trip. I had sincerely tapped a hidden waterspout of Heaven, and in it was that language. I thanked the priest for allowing me to borrow the church, and he graciously accepted, with one request, that I should return to give a report on my trip. I did return later and gave him and his Bible-study group a glowing report.

That summer (1979), I had a most amazing trip. Every footstep was ordered of God. He put me into a river of praise at that little church that then carried me to an ocean of divine connections in the glory. Realizing that praise kept me flowing with Him, I arose each morning of the trip at 6:00 am to sing in tongues. This also brought to me the ability to speak better Italian at each intersection of the trip.

I met the man who carved the Nobel prize medal. I also met the mother superior of the order of Poor Clare nuns for the Fransiscans in Assisi. We spent an afternoon together in her garden discussing the baptism of the Holy Ghost.

In Rome, we met Padre Martini, the official Vatican Artist, a born-again Franciscan monk, who showed us his famous studio on the Tiber River. While gazing over the veranda upon the sunset of Rome, I was surprised when our host suddenly whipped the stem of a magnificent potted fern around my wrist, bringing my hand up in front of my face. He said, "You will never create a masterpiece until you know the Master who created it all. Know God!" Father Martini clearly knew Him. I recalled this years later when my painting was hung next to one by the master artist Rembrandt.

A chief Vatican musician took me to the Pope's office to pray over his chair. We got tickets for an audience and attended. In the evening, I joined him and some of his choir to sing a cappella on the steps of St. Peter's Cathedral. We sang down the walls that separated our denominations. Crashing waves of glory destroyed them, and Jesus was magnified.

We were thrilled, in 1999, when Father Tom Di Lorenzo of the Boston area assisted us with our revival meetings on Cape Cod, Massachusetts. Our regional coordinator, Pastor Steve Johnson of Living Waters Christian Center, contacted him in reaching out to all of the Christian leaders of the area. He brought with him a very large group (nearly two hundred of his people), and they filled a great section of the auditorium, along with the Pentecostal, Charismatic and Protestant believers.

It is good to see God's people in harmony. It grieves the Holy Spirit to see us at war with one another. If you are a general in one of these "holy wars," beware. An ocean wave may be headed your way. God uses His forces on the gates that have locked out part of His people. He is not happy with anything that stops the flow of His love.

These same "holy wars" have raged between Pentecostals and Baptists. God loves them both, and it is time for each side to love the other as well.

Has any man ever had absolutely perfect theology? Only God can judge, and He will have a word for us as we pass through the gates of Heaven. On that day, not only our beliefs will be tested, but every word we have uttered will be judged. We must be sure that our words are golden. The true sign of those who lead in the next revival of this century will be their gracious ability to love those of other sects and denominations within the faith.

 The true sign of those who lead in the next revival of this century will be their gracious ability to love those of other sects and denominations within the faith.

When I went to Russia in 1987, I was in a mixed, Evangelical and Orthodox, group. The Orthodox in the group were monks who were going to Russia for the purpose of visiting some of the revered Orthodox monasteries there. The rest of us were more interested in underground churches. The New York tour company that arranged the trip had mistakenly put the two groups together, not realizing how very different our interests were.

It seemed like an impossible marriage, but we were stuck with each other, so we decided to make the best of it. In this way, we were able to visit some of the Orthodox monasteries of Russia — something we might not have done otherwise.

In one particular monastery, a guide told us something that was very challenging to our beliefs. Praying people, she said, had often come and stood before the icons in trances that lasted for hours at a time. This would disturb the evangelicals who have observed much darkness over that land, where the Bible was banned for seventy years. A void of the Word quite often permits an opening for the deceiving work of familiar spirits.

But if we were dirt poor, had no education and lived in a Communist country where God was considered to be an illegal alien, might we have tried to reach God like this too? My friend Dwight Jones of Vision for the Nations in Caddo Mills, Texas, preaches a sermon entitled, "Desperation Precedes Revelation."

Icons were originally introduced to tell Bible stories to illiterate people through pictures. Stained glass windows evolved the same way. Using them as a point of contact is not a problem, but the veneration or worship of them is. Today we have illustrated Bibles and photos of our popular Christian preachers and singers. The ancients painted theirs. We too must not idolize anyone or anything above Christ. God can use anything that is pure, and the pure in heart shall see Him.

 Desperation precedes revelation!

The Spirit of God was travailing for Russia and the Russian people. There can be no doubt about that fact. So, did He use icons to reach them? We can't say for sure, but we can say that He once wrote words of judgment on the wall of a king's palace with His own finger as a graphic sign to warn that king to repent.

One of Rembrandt's paintings of that biblical story hangs next to my *The Travail of the Flag* in the Sacred Arts Center at Great Passion Play in Eureka Springs, Arkansas. I have seen the painting many times and feel it is significant that the two hang together. There are two reasons. First, it is an answer to a prayer I prayed when I was just fourteen years old. As I stood in front of the great Louvre museum in Paris, I dedicated my life to God. I said, "Lord, if You will teach me to paint like these great masters, I will serve You all my life." Now, my art keeps company with Titian's and Rembrandt's. Secondly, knowing that the two paintings hang side by side thrills me because both of them illustrate the fact that God does indeed use graphic images and signs to warn nations.

My Evangelical friends on that Russian trip didn't know it, but I had spent a year in study with an Orthodox church before becoming an Evangelical. Because of that, I was hearing the guide differently than they were. I was hearing her as a student of Orthodoxy. I also heard the guide as a child of a Roman Catholic father and a Presbyterian mother who had loved each other despite their differences, had respected each other's preferences and had lived together as man and wife in the same house for years. Of all the couples I had known in my lifetime, my parents were still some of the most secure in their relationship. Our home was always a melting pot for many and extended the same warm hospitality to everyone. Yes, I was hearing our guide from a totally different perspective.

Later that same day, when I joined an Orthodox priest in song as we rode along on a train bound for Moscow, some members of both groups were shocked. He was singing some of the old anthems of the faith. They were songs on the blood of our covenant salvation. Stanzas of the great song *"Holy God, Holy Mighty One, Holy Immortal God, Have Mercy"* lilted through our car. The priests had not considered that anyone in our group was knowledgable of their faith, and I hadn't told anyone in our group that I was knowledgable of theirs. God had reserved the moment.

Later, I once sang this song in a church where I testified about the trip. Someone made the comment that it brought to mind the heaviness of religion without power. A scripture immediately came to my mind:

> *Let us then approach the throne of grace with confidence, so that we may receive mercy and find grace to help us in our time of need.*
> Hebrews 4:16, NIV

We cannot usher in the glory apart from mercy. Does this present generation not need mercy? Is there nothing for which we need to come boldly to God? To the contrary, if it were not for the mercy of God, our world would be nearly as bad off as Sodom and Gomorrah.

The Hebrew scriptural phrase *"Qui tov. Qui Le olam hasto"* (The Lord is good. His mercy endureth forever) shows the connection between mercy and glory. As this phrase was sung at the dedication of Solomon's Temple, the glory fell so that the priests could no longer stand to minister. Hebrew scholar Rev. Billye Brim teaches: *"Tov* simply means 'good.' *Qui Le olam hasto* means 'His mercy endureth forever.' Glory and goodness are related by God's showing His goodness when Moses had asked to see His glory. The full supply of 'goodness-mercy,' *tov,* is heavyladen blessing. It is weighty." [1]

In crying for mercy, we usher in the glory and power. The cry of the old Orthodox hymn is actually very scriptural. So, why would anyone automatically associate it with powerless religion and familiar spirits? Is it because it isn't in our modern hymnals?

God Almighty loves that song, and it was not written for us to criticize! Angels sing it in Heaven around the throne of God, and when we get there, we may just become "stuck in place" with them, frozen in awe for millions of years, singing this song as we gaze upon the most unfathomable sight of God's throne and Him upon it. We will all be astonished and cry, "Holy!"

All the questions we have wanted to ask Him will flee from our minds in that moment, and our theology will suddenly be seen for what it lacked, especially in love. As Sister Ruth Ward Heflin told me (while I stayed with her in August of 1998 praying on assignment for our president, in his hour of crisis), "Let us err on the side of mercy, rather than judgment." God's Word teaches us, *"Let every man be swift to hear, slow to speak, slow to wrath [anger]"* (James 1:19, NKJ).

 "Let us err on the side of mercy, rather than judgment."

Jesus has saints in every river and every camp, and there are also some "hangers-on." In His own little group, Jesus had a Judas, but He never treated the man unkindly. Let us love and encourage all of God's children, and let us not be quick to discount a miracle just because it came forth for a sinner or for other Christians with whom we are unfamiliar.

For my own part, I visit all sorts of Christian groups, and when I am asked to preach, I count it a joy. I find that God is ready to bless all men everywhere — if they will only reach out to Him.

With cults, of course, we must deal differently. We can love them, but we cannot embrace or encourage their practices. Cults usually demand works and promote uncertainty about salvation. They do not honor the Bible as the Word of God. Jesus is not God or Lord to them. They don't believe in the Trinity. Some church leader is usually a higher authority than the Bible. Most often, the fruit of these cults is bad. They honor an experience that leads them away from the Word of God.

We must keep our definitions of a cult simple so that we can help many who are trying to take the limitations off of their fellowship with Christians who may be different from them. We must allow God's *Oceans of Glory* to flood His entire Bride with the love that will cause the whole world to know that we are *"one"* in Him.

A group of people who belong to one group that mainline Christians commonly classify as a cult came to hear me do a drama on the crucifixion of Jesus in 1993. I was employed at the time by The Great Passion Play Outdoor Holy Land Theme Park. So great was the anointing on the program that the entire group was dumbfounded. They could not get back on their bus, but just stood there weeping.

Finally, their elder asked me if I would sing again and play my harp. I did, but they still would not move.

At last, he stepped forward. He had a clipboard and pen in his hand. Very humbly, he asked me, "Excuse me, ma'am, but we don't think we have ever heard anything like that before."

"Which part?" I asked.

"The part about the blood," he said. "Um ... do you think you could come and preach for us?"

I said I would be happy to do it, and he wrote down my name and contact information.

I prayed for the group before they left, sensing that their leaders back home would never let them invite me to come. The message of salvation by the cleansing, forgiving blood of Jesus was not part of their foundation. I do believe, however, that I will see some of those folks in Heaven one day because they believed my message on salvation. I was glad I hadn't judged them. By God's grace and mercy, I had loved them, and they had responded eagerly.

God is moving in many unlikely places, places that we would not choose — if the decision were left to us. Let us take the limits off of God and let Him use us where He will. We might as well do it because when His *Oceans of Glory* come sweeping in, they will eradicate all artificial barriers anyway. Then the prayer of Jesus will be answered, *"That they may be one."*

 We must allow God's *Oceans of Glory* to flood His entire Bride with the love that will cause the whole world to know that we are *"one"* in Him.

ENDNOTE

1. From a tape series, "The Goodness of God," the year 2000, Prayer Mountain of the Ozarks, Branson, Missouri.

FIFTEEN

CHASE THE WAVE

They that go down to the sea in ships, that do business in great waters;
These see the works of the LORD, and his wonders in the deep.
Psalm 107:23-24

The river has a current, but the ocean has a rhythm. Heaven's population sings it continuously, day and night, around the throne of God. "Holy! Holy! Holy!" When there is an opening between the pulsating of "Holy, holy, holy," like the mitral-valve of a heart, grab the miracles. A finely tuned ear pressed to Jesus' bosom in prayer can hear that sound. The key is pressing in.

A few days before our 1993 Pillars of Fire meeting, a friend invited us to preach in Tulsa, Oklahoma. Due to a tight schedule, I started to decline, but the Spirit said, "Go." So we went.

In Tulsa, we set up a life-sized copy of *The Travail of the Flag* mural, the vision for blood-bought revival in America that God inspired me to paint in 1987. I used it to illustrate a sermon. Afterward, I turned to hand my hostess the microphone. Then, suddenly and inexplicably, it seemed that I had simply stepped into a wall of God. His presence froze me ... and everyone else (to one degree or another), during many minutes of silence all over the room.

It was a startling experience in the glory, like none I had before. It seemed that my entire life, and especially the ministry, flashed before me, coming up due for a curtain call, a final examination, before the presence of the all-consuming, all-knowing, all-seeing Almighty God.

In that moment, there was not a sermon, a painting, a song, a mission trip or any other thing that I could find to present as evidence of successfully answering His call on my life. All that I had done until that moment was as dust scattered to the wind, uncollectible, out of my grasp to reassemble or bring before Him as something well done. I stood before Him with nothing. NOTHING!

So overwhelming was God's presence in that moment, that it was not even possible to recollect my own name. My thoughts were scrambled, and I was numb. All awareness of others in the room was also gone.

Instantly, I was reminded of just how fearful it would be to fall into the hands of the living God without the blood of Jesus, the Christ.

Aha! The blood of Jesus ... Suddenly I did remember it! My eyes opened and settled upon the mural before us. In fact, my eyes were fused to it, as God began to speak to me. He said: "You have run this race seven years. You have preached on the blood, and that was good. You have preached on the end times and the patriotic roots of your nation." (These were the three inherent messages in the mural.) "But," the Lord said, "you have not yet hit the main vein."

Rebuked and stunned, I asked, "What is that, Lord?"

He led me to gaze intently upon the mural, and it did not seem to belong to me at all. It was more like a baby that suddenly had strong legs to run on its own.

As I stared at the image, it seemed that the circle of blood, fire and water flowing from Christ's side, encircling the American continent and then back across nations in the mural, began to come to life and swirl around America. The Spirit narrated for me what I was seeing:

"Behold the blood and the glory, how they encircle the globe and particularly swirl around your nation! It is the will of God that EVERY man, woman and child in America find his or her audience with God and stay there until he or she abides in His presence in the place of His power."

Then He lifted me up, as if one would rise rapidly in a rocket to the heavens above our continent. In a bird's-eye view, I saw America and Canada and places aglow on the map. I heard laughter in all those places.

Then the Lord spoke: "Do you hear the sound of laughter, My daughter?" I answered affirmatively. He continued, "It is the happy sound of My children — silly, giddy, romping in the first foam of the first wave. It is not yet the sound of revival."

I sensed God's divine pleasure in all of this but also understood His yearning for more for us. It reminded me of a father driving his children to a beach when they had never seen the ocean. Before he can fully park on the sand and warn them not to run into traffic, to use their life preservers or to avoid the riptide, they are already off and running into the breakers, having fun. What can he do but just enjoy their pleasure? It's a pleasant scene, but the Lord wants more of us.

I asked, "Lord, then what is *the* sound of revival?"

Then I saw a cloud move over this nation. It settled upon hot glowing spots in the Great Lakes region, Florida and the Midwest, and it filled in all the gaps in between. As this happened, hordes of peoples were slain in the Spirit as one would be pressed to the bottom beneath the weight of an ocean. Then the Lord said, "Some will come laughing. Some will come shouting. Some will come screaming. [I sensed this to be as they suddenly would come in contact with the glory unawares.] And some will come slain in the Spirit for days."

"How many days, Lord?" I asked.

"For days," He repeated.

The depth of that answer echoed like the deep sounding of leagues of ocean water. It seemed that the length of days under which these masses will be slain will surpass anything our present minds or historical experiences can comprehend. It will perhaps be as great as a week of days, exceeding the things documented in the turn-of-the-twentieth-century revivals. "DAYS!"

Again, I asked the Lord, "How many days?"

"For days. I will get them any way I can get them, but I will get them." It was a sovereignly sealed matter.

Then He allowed me to see what I believe was the final move of His Spirit in Texas. I saw sparks shooting out from that state — northward, eastward, westward and southward.

 "For days. I will get them any way I can get them, BUT I WILL GET THEM."

I saw a young man slain on the carpet. He could have been an usher, businessman, Bible school student or preacher, because he was dressed in a suit and seemed very sharp in his appearance. The glory of God seemed to "sit" heavily upon him, so he could not get up and run away. He was moaning and writhing, almost as if in pain. I came close and heard his struggle, as he spoke to the Lord: "No! Oh, no, Lord! How will I ever give up that one thing? You can't ask me to do it. It's a perfectly good thing, not evil. How can I ever manage... ?"

Eventually, after a period of struggle, he and God somehow came to a working-out of this final issue, and he became free and full of the Holy Ghost, ready for unhindered service. God sovereignly did what the young man could never have done by himself in resolving the matter.

At this point, the young man burst up off the floor, and so did masses of others, and I suddenly heard the sound of thundering feet. Hordes of cleansed, filled, anointed, holy believers stampeded to the mission fields of the earth, into everyman's world, in a last, quick, great harvest thrust.

The Lord concluded the visitation, "This is *the* sound of revival." Then I came back to myself and the room of ministers ... and the silence.

"Slain in the Spirit of the Lord for days" ... Jesus, the voice of prophecy, spoke it to me in 1993, as the first wave of revival was breaking around the globe at the close of the twentieth century. It would carry us on into the new century and only increase from that point on. The Holy Spirit was preparing me for the duration of the movement, giving a preview of what was to follow.

How nice it was to have a road map so that we would not become side-tracked or lost! This vision helped me to pace myself in the midst of a scurry of revival outbreaks. I was able to minister some, while, at the same time, attend some meetings to prepare myself so that our ministry could be ready for the tsunami that I sensed was coming.

This word from God helped me to avoid the pitfalls of hysteria over one particular manifestation versus another. It caused me to be flexible and understand that we are not to camp out and stay only with the manifestation of shaking or laughing, or with the sign of "gold dust" or some other. All of this was wonderful, but it was not yet the fullness of the revival. That is yet to come. These things were but the foam of the first waves to break upon us.

In the spring of 1999, I began to hear a restless stir in congregations of many churches where we ministered. Pastors let us know that the "river" was no longer flowing in the same way that it had been. Some parishioners were disillusioned and leaving in search of greater manifestations of glory. Others were blaming the pastors for easing up on the revival mode and demanding that the manifestations continue as before — as if pastors could control it. Thank God, we helped some by sharing this 1993 vision.

It was not time to leave their churches, I told them, but to realize that the pause had been orchestrated by God. A huge influx of new converts had come into His Kingdom in those waves, and many saints had returned and been refreshed. There were many needs among the people.

As I observed God's people at worship in many places, they were rejoicing together, grateful that the house, or sanctuary, was filled with warm bodies. I noticed that most of our music was on a celebration level, a horizontal level. Its tone was sometimes still earthly, carnal. The mood was often: "Aren't we having fun? You're here, and I'm here. Whoopee!"

All of this was (and is still) great. Praise God for it. But now, it is time for us all to grow up. We need to press in to a new worship level, one with a vertical direction (earth to the throne room), and many are doing just that. We need to enjoy the brief calm and listen to the teaching of God's Word to *"study to show [ourselves] approved."*

Many have no fruit developed in their soulish realm, not yet knowing how to walk in love. They have not learned how to manage a checkbook or fix their marriage and home life. They need to develop soul-winning skills, and if they are not taught to pray, the ol' devil will soon "devour their lunch" (see 1 Corinthians 3:2).

Even some new ministers need further maturing. I have met many ministers in the past decade of revival who have no ethics. They often say that they will be somewhere at a certain time, and then they don't show up. They need to learn how to swear to their own hurt and possess their vessel and gift properly.

The pause in the river has brought us to a junction where we enter the channels of deep water. We may change equipment and even crews. Navigation charts must be checked. The current flows differently out in the deeper water, and the Church is now moving to a new level.

Children who love playing in ankle-deep water will be sad when the wave recedes. The tow is strong. Some stand still and weep, and others are knocked off balance. But some run and chase the wave into the drying ocean bed, further and further out toward the water's foamy, receding edge. [1]

Suddenly, the wave returns, and another one comes after it. Instantly, they are submerged, not ankle deep, but over their heads. (This is important, for some need their brains baptized.) In the depths, they now stand, having chased a wave far from the dry shore, and they are submerged, surfacing again in glee. They have found deep waters to swim in!

 The current flows differently out in the deeper water, and the Church is now moving to a new level.

This is what is happening to our revival in America and elsewhere. The water has merely pulled back for a short season. Those who crave it and chase it will suddenly be pleasantly rewarded in the depth of the next wave. Churches that have comprehended this pattern are not diminishing, but prayer groups are forming within them, and the congregations are maintaining steady membership, preparing to rush in with the tidal waves that soon will break down the seawalls of closed cities destined for revival.

We will next see God open the last barred gates for China's millions of people. Ronnie and I ministered eight days to her communist leaders in 1992 and shall never forget our parting meal. After we resisted toasting whiskey with one official from Beijing, he, having lost diplomatic control and in an attempt to restore the fragile etiquette, demanded that I, instead, sing to entertain them. Instantly, the Holy Spirit overwhelmed me, until I appeared "drunk" with laughter.

"What shall we sing?" I replied. Not knowing what to suggest, he helplessly accepted my invitation to join us as we sang together: "Jesus loves me, this I know, for the Bible tells me so" (this, in the land that barred the Bible). Pleased, the man clapped vigorously and surprised us when he said, "I love Christmas carols. Sing it again!" We did, and so shall all of China!

In 1989, the world awoke one morning to a long-awaited, but suddenly realized event. The Berlin Wall had fallen, and the Iron Curtain that had withheld freedom and the Gospel from so many was but a vapor in the winds of history. God's "suddenlies" are awesome, because, like a tsunami, they catch us unawares.

Prior to such an event, God is always preparing a people to be ready to harness the power of the wave of glory He sends forth. They are a people of faith who paddle the oars of their canoes upstream against the normal flow of life, pausing with a listening ear to catch the faint whirl of the falls in the distance, a place of sudden change. Led by the Spirit of God, they are in a position to avoid catastrophes and receive great blessing.

> *"He who has an ear, let him hear what the Spirit says to the churches."*
> Revelation 3:22, NIV

Let us not he disheartened or slack in our spiritual stance in these days. Press in to God as never before. Believe for the coming *Oceans of Glory*, and begin now to chase the wave. We are going to new levels. [2]

Are we ready for the oceans? Ready or not, here they come!

Tsunami!

ENDNOTES

1. There is a great book on this subject: *The River of God* by Rev. Beth Barnes, P.O. Box 34426, Indianapolis, IN 40234.
2. I was thrilled with the recent exhortations of Phil Derstine of Christian Retreat Center in Bradenton, Florida, to all ministers desiring revival to press to a new level.

APPENDICES

A Visit to Hell

Jesus saith unto him, I am the way, the truth, and the life: no man cometh unto the Father, but by me.   John 14:6

Hell is a horrible place. I went there briefly in 1970 as a young teenager, and I never want to see the place again. It happened in this way (due to an overdose of prescription drugs that could well have killed me):

In the middle of the night, I awoke to a state of total blindness and found that I was also dumb. No one in the house could hear my feeble screams. In my panic, I pulled out a dental brace that I wore after school and ripped open a cut on the inside of both cheeks. The flow of blood suddenly let me know that I was still alive.

I may have been alive, but I was certainly not out of danger. Just at that moment, I became aware of a terrible sucking force pulling at me. It was pulling me down ... down ... down into the very depths of the earth. There, I found myself in utter darkness and solitude, and a familiar voice began to mock me.

I recognized the voice as that of one of my classmates from high school, a girl who had been insistently inviting me to the smoking lounge every day. Now she was taunting me, "Come on, Shelli, let's party in Hell together!" But as I reached out for her, she faded away, as if in some sort of echo chamber.

My whole life began to flash before me. First, I saw my mother's face. I was a toddler in her arms, looking up at her in the rocking chair, as she sang softly to me before my nap time. I reached up to touch her cheek, and she, too, was gone. Something told me that I would never see her again if I stayed in that hellish state of being.

Suddenly, I simply could not bear that thought. Then I realized that in that place I would never feel the touch of any other human hand again. There would be no more partying — with anyone "together." I was in the loneliest place in all the universe.

Do you remember the rich man and Lazarus, and how the rich man had begged Jesus for just one more opportunity to go back and warn his friends and family members not to go there? How sad that an unsuspecting world would someday face this end! How could I have been so foolish?

When I realized that the light of day would never dawn on me again where I was, I began to cry, for my heart was suddenly terrorized. "Oh God," I cried. "Have mercy. Save me!" The words seemed to echo through the nothingness of my private Hell.

Then the thought of all thoughts struck my soul like lightning. It was not from the words of any evangelist I had ever heard; I was receiving a revelation in Hell: "If I never see the light of day again, then I shall never see the face of my God who created me!" This, too, was more than I could bear. I suddenly realized that every agnostic, satanist, and atheist would believe in God — once they had experienced Hell.

Then, the miracle I sought came. God answered my anguished cry, and I heard a voice that shook that place: *"I am the way, the truth and the life. Follow Me!"*

A pinhole of light appeared, and another force like a vacuum, this one with an upward pull, sucked me up out of there. I felt much like a drowning victim who had been thrown a rope and pulled into a passing ship. I was not going to drown after all; I was being rescued. I was not going to live eternally in darkness after all; I was safe. I was not going to live without love or comfort forever. God loved me.

My eyes opened and I looked around. I was in my own room and in my own bed. I threw myself gratefully out of the bed and began to cry out to God for salvation. I wasn't sure of His identity yet. A whole list of names flowed from my lips: Buddah, Mohammed, Jesus. At the first, there was no answer, but the name of Jesus brought back memories from childhood of bedtime prayers and seemed very right. Although I wasn't sure I knew the exact way I should pray, He heard me.

Two weeks later a friend, Jayne Irye, of the Presbyterian Church in Churchville, Maryland, witnessed to me at a covered-dish supper: "If you died tonight, where would you go?" That night, when I went home, Mother was folding laundry while she watched a Billy Graham crusade on television. I sat down to listen.

The dryer buzzer rang, and when Mother left the room to gather another load of clothes, I jumped up to turn the dial to one of my favorite programs. Just then, Dr. Graham said, "Do not touch that dial! You could be in church every Sunday, but if you do not know Jesus, you will spend eternity in Hell. [I knew that he was talking to me.] You must know Him, not from holiday to holiday or Sunday to Sunday, but from heartbeat to heartbeat." That day, I prayed the sinner's prayer and was saved right there in my own living room.

I never want to see Hell again, and it pains me to think of others going there. How can we avoid it ourselves and help others to avoid it? We must allow God's *Oceans of Glory* to sweep over this sin-sick world!

My Prayer for You

If you need the Lord, dear reader, you can find Him today. His Word speaks to you now:

Jesus declared, "I tell you the truth, no one can see the kingdom of God unless he is born again." John 3:3, NIV

Marvel not that I said unto thee, Ye must be born again. John 3:7

For God so loved the world, that he gave his only begotten Son, that whosoever believeth in him should not perish, but have everlasting life. John 3:16

Jesus saith unto him, I am the way, the truth, and the life: no man cometh unto the Father, but by me. John 14:6

For all have sinned, and come short of the glory of God. Romans 3:23

That if thou shalt confess with thy mouth the Lord Jesus, and shalt believe in thine heart that God hath raised him from the dead, thou shalt be saved. For with the heart man believeth unto righteousness; and with the mouth confession is made unto salvation. For the scripture saith, Whosoever believeth on him shall not be ashamed. Romans 10:9-11

If you would like to accept His invitation, please pray this prayer with me:

Almighty God, Creator of the Universe,
I pray that I, a sinner, may be heard — through the sacrifice of the blood of Your Son, Jesus. I thank You, Jesus, for dying on the cross for me. Thank You for paying the price for my sins. I know that without Your mercy I would remain a sinner and go to an eternal Hell. Even my best works are not good enough to take me to Heaven, where Your perfection and glory reign. Thank

You for having mercy on me. Now, Lord, please forgive my sins and become the Lord of my life. I want to serve You and go to Heaven with You and see the Kingdom of God.

Amen!

Now, friend, if you prayed that prayer, or in your own words cried out to God for His help, I believe that what He has promised in His Word has now come to pass in you. If you have confessed Jesus as your Savior, you are now born again. Believe it and act upon it.

Welcome into the Kingdom of God. I encourage you now to press in to a life of prayer in the Lord, to read your Bible and attend church. In this way, you will be daily refreshed from above and inspired to follow the leading of the Holy Spirit in your own heart into His perfect will for your life.

If there is any other way we can be of service to you, please don't hesitate to contact us at our ministry address.

OCEAN SCRIPTURES

There are many wonderful scriptures related to the oceans. Here are a few of them:

Genesis 1:1-4 and 6-10
Job 28:25-28
Psalms 24:1-6, 33:7-11, 36:5-10, 46:3, 65:7-11, 89:9, 93:3-4 and 139:9-12
Proverbs 8:22-33
Isaiah 40:12 and 64:2
Jeremiah 5:22
Ezekiel 31:15
Haggai 2:6
Zechariah 10:1
Revelation 17:15, 19:6, 20:13 and 21:1

Although they are wonderful in all versions of the Bible, the word *oceans* appears in each of them only in The Living Bible (except for Zechariah 10:1).

Ministry address:

Harvest Projects International
P.O. Box 177
Branson, MO 65615

Fax: 417-348-1719

harvestprojects@cfaith.com
shellibake@aol.com
http://members.aol.com/shellibake/index.html
www.harvestprojects.com

We have many wonderful testimonies of healing and deliverance from the people we mention in the book whom God has blessed in our meetings. If you would enjoy reading them, please visit our websites and be encouraged in your faith.